Total Resistance

H. Von Dach

Cover Design: J.Neuman

www.snowballpublishing.com
info@snowballpublishing.com

For information regarding special discounts for bulk purchases, please contact Snowball Publishing at sales@snowballpublishing.com

CONTENTS

ACKNOWLEDGEMENTS

I wish to take this opportunity to thank those individuals who assisted me in preparing this manuscript for publication. Special thanks goes to our linguist, Hans Lienhard who presently is attached to the Special Warfare Language Facility, Special Warfare Center, Fort Bragg, North Carolina. William and Mary Jones, Vice-President and Editorial Assistant respectively for PANTHER PUBLICATIONS provided both encouragement and advice in editing the translation as well as administering the business while I was on active duty. Dr. Louis Soens, presently teaching English Literature at Notre Dame and Dr. Walter O'Donnell, member of the English Department at the University of Colorado, were extremely helpful in proof reading the edited translation and providing editorial comment.

R.K.B.

Resistance to the Last

Let us assume the following: Switzerland has become a battlefield. Superior enemy forces have invaded the country. Here and there our troops have been overrun. However, many have succeeded in evading the enemy. They are still in possession of their weapons and equipment. They want to fight, resist to the last. But how?

Or: The enemy has occupied a city. The population is under his rule. What does the worker, the employee, the self-employed do in such a case? What does the teacher, the newspaper editor, the doctor, the state employee do? What about housewives, railroad employees, postal employees, and policemen?

What do the soldiers do? What do the civilians do?

Will some throw away their weapons since they believe continued resistance is futile?

Will others wait for the future, placing their faith in God, or will they cooperate with the enemy?

So many questions—but where are the answers?

One thing is certain. The enemy will show no mercy. The enemy will snuff out one life, dozens, hundreds or thousands without any qualms if this would further his aims. The captured soldier will face deportation, forced labor or death. But so will the worker, the employee, the self-employed, and the housewife.

The enemy will not make any distinction between soldiers and civilians. Experiences of the recent past have proved that annihilation of the conquered may be expected sooner or later. Sometimes, this process is only delayed.

The officer, the noncommissioned officer, the teacher, the editor—each individual who, at one time or another, has made any derogatory remarks about the ideology of the enemy, who, before the war, stood up for democracy and liberty and vocally opposed dictatorship and despotism—all these will lead the deportation and liquidation list. This we must understand!

What then must be done when the enemy is in the country? What has to be done in view of the certainty that danger and death will threaten each citizen, male or female, regardless of whether he wants to play an active or passive role?

We believe it is better to resist until the last. We believe that every Swiss woman or man must resist. We believe that the enemy cannot be allowed to feel at ease for even one minute in the conquered territory. We believe that we have to inflict damage upon him, fight him wherever and whenever we have the opportunity! By speaking this way we have clearly and explicitly indicated the purpose of this book.

In case of war, resistance will come primarily through the Army. It is our duty to make-sure with our might that the Army is and remains ready for war. We want this point understood very clearly.

However, we want to show our people a way to resist in case parts of the Army are dispersed, split up or encircled. This is in case prisoners succeed in escaping or portions of the civilian population fall under enemy rule. We want to demonstrate that in the worst situation resistance is not in vain, but that it is a primary duty.

We feel this book will make this resistance effective, that it will prevent bloodshed and loss of life because of lack of necessary know-how and ability.

Perhaps one might say that it is wrong and unwise to discuss these things publicly, to write about them and to inform a potential enemy of what we intend to do should he attack us. We do not believe in this concept. On the contrary, we believe that, because of our openly demonstrated will to resist to the last, the enemy will have one more factor to consider when evaluating the 'pros' and 'cons' of a planned "Operation Switzerland."

We publish this book with this in mind and hope that it will find thousands of readers.

The Central Committee of the
Swiss Noncommissioned Officers Association

INTRODUCTION BY WENDELL W. FERTIG, COLONEL USA - RET.

(Colonel Fertig organized and commanded the Philippine-American guerrilla forces on Mindanao after the fall of the Philippines. During three years of Japanese occupation he developed them into a highly trained and effective force of some 35,000. His efforts did much to pave the way for the return of the American forces to Mindanao in 1945. After the war, Fertig served as Consultant for Guerrilla and Monetary Affairs to U.S. High Commissioner McNutt. In 1951, he was assigned to the Special Forces Division, Office of Psychological Warfare at the Pentagon where he played an important role in establishing the Special Forces Center at Fort Bragg, N.C. In 1953, he spent several months studying counter guerrilla operations against the Huks in the Philippines; then with the French in Indo-China and with General Templar's forces in Malaya. Col. Fertig retired in 1956 but has continued as a consultant in guerrilla warfare and counterinsurgency for the government and has lectured on said subjects at the Air University and the Air Force Academy. Recently Colonel Fertig joined Panther Publication's Advisory Board as a consultant.)

To comment on this book is difficult unless it is considered as a text book or Field Manual devoted to the specialized problems of Civilian Resistance and their solution. The illustrations are superb and the text explicit. It is a how-to-do-it manual in a field that has been long neglected; i.e. what courses of action are open to civilians who reside in an area occupied by a foreign aggressor. In case of enemy occupation, it is generally assumed that the civilians will resist. How such resistance is to be implimented or sustained is left up to the individual who is usually at a complete loss as to what to do. With the publication of TOTAL RESISTANCE this is no longer the case as this book spells out the when, where and how of developing and organizing guerrilla bands, a civilian resistance movement and an underground.

Specific comments seem to be in order as there is no sustained story to review. The first of these comments touches a place dear to my heart. Among all the famous resistance efforts tabulated the guerrilla warfare in the Philippines goes unmentioned. Yet this was a resistance that sprang from the people and was carried on for five months behind the Japanese lines before receiving recognition or help from the Allies. From this experience came the basis for the concept and policy of the U.S. Special Forces.

A resistance that can be organized and sustained early in the occupation has the best chance of surviving. It must be organized before the enemy can institute the block control system in cities, and while some unrestricted movement is possible in the country areas. Further it must be remembered that the most successful guerrilla movements have always been based on areas that are isolated by terrain, poor roads and bad weather. Operations within a city are difficult. The Warsaw uprising was an exception and this was possible because of ghetto conditions that will not be found in other cities. Even there, the real effectiveness of the uprising was destroyed when it was tricked into premature attacks on the Germans, while the Russians awaited the mutual destruction of both adversaries.

Secrecy is imperative. It is almost impossible to maintain but often can be better achieved through the use of misleading rumors than through tight security. To provide the enemy with several stories, all of which require interpretation and decision, will often provide the time needed to carry out an operation.

In my command in the Philippines, I found that the only way to break out of an ambush action was to provide indigenous personnel with limited ammunition. A guerrilla with an empty rifle will retreat readily, while one with an adequate supply of ammunition will stay too long and risk capture.

Medicines are frequently the best means of financing any type of resistance. The individual items are easily carried. As an example, thirty atabrine tablets would take a courier further than thirty thousand Japanese occupation pesos, and with much less risk of discovery.

In preparation for issuing currency of your own, the adequate supply of paper and ink are very important. The enemy will attempt to control the supplies of these items, thus negating any possibility of providing an alternate system of currency.

One need that is most important and which is mentioned but not stressed, is the need of an organization within the Prisoner of War or Concentration Camps. The basic organization should be provided before the surrender takes place. The lack of this planning was responsible for uncounted deaths in POW camps in the Philippines. Divide and rule by the enemy lead to the break down of all command authority and the prisoners were at the mercy of the Japanese guards. In Singapore, the Australian troops entered the POW camp with a table of organization and command. They were able to present a united front toward their captors and fared better than the American POW's who did not have such an organization.

These comments do not lessen the impact of this fine manual which is the first ever published that not only describes the practices of the Communists but offers methods for opposing their oppressive rule. It is interesting to note that the Swiss Noncommissioned Officers Association is able to point where the dangers lay and how they may be met.

In all of this, it is well to repeat six basic principles which must be present if such a resistance is to succeed and eventual victory be achieved. These are:

1. A loyal people who will support the effort at great risk to themselves.
2. Favorable terrain, and organization to fit particular terrain needs. A possible safe haven.
3. A source of adequate finances.
4. Good communications (radio, telephone, etc.)
5. An adequate supply of food to support the units.
6. Support from an outside power (most important).

The final paragraphs of the book bear repeating here. "If two enemies fight each other to the last—and this is always the case where an ideology is involved (religion is part of it) guerrilla warfare and civilian resistance will inevitably break out in the final phase.

"The military expert who undervalues or even disregards guerrilla warfare makes a mistake since he does not take into consideration the strength of heart.

"The last, and admittedly, most cruel battle will be fought by civilians. It will be conducted under the fear of deportation, of execution, and concentration camps.

"We must and will win this battle since each Swiss male and female in particular believe in the innermost part of their hearts—even if they are too shy and sober in everyday life to admit or even speak about it—in the old, and yet very up-to-date saying:

Death rather than slavery!"

Wendell W. Fertig
Colonel USA - Ret.

Introduction

The author is fully aware of the fact that he has touched upon a difficult and unpleasant subject. Nevertheless, in the age of total warfare where not only material but also ideological factors are at stake, it is imperative to discuss these problems.

It may be assumed that in case of a war, large areas—if not all—of our territory will be temporarily lost to the enemy. The Army may be largely neutralized even though sizeable units should continue to fight for an extended period in the Alpine regions.

However, the majority of the soldiers as well as the masses of the civilian populace will survive the campaign. Now comes the question—should these survivors become loyal subjects of the new rulers, waiting for salvation and liberation from the outside, or should the fight be continued in a new manner with all available means?

It may be assumed that with the well known love for freedom of the population on the one hand and the proven ruthlessness of the potential enemy on the other, clashes between the occupation forces and the conquered will sooner or later become inevitable. Thus it may not be entirely useless to write about the atmosphere, tactics and techniques of guerrilla warfare as far as these can be reconstructed from the experiences of past wars from the Spanish guerrillas fighting against Napoleon to the French Maquis of World War II.

The Author

The Most Important Guerrilla Actions of the Past and the Present

- The actions in the Vendée during the French revolution
- The Spanish guerrillas fighting against Napoleon
- The uprising in Tyrol against Napoleon
- Guerrilla operations in Central Germany against Napoleon (raiding parties)
- Greek liberation operations against the Turks
- Guerrilla operations during the Franco-Prussian War of 1870/71
- Austrian "Pacification operations" in Bosnia
- Activities of Belgian insurgents of 1914
- German Army cavalry raids behind French lines during 1914
- Serbian insurgent operations during World War I
- Lawrence's desert operations against the Turks during World War I
- Activities of resistance fighters in the occupied Ruhr area after World War I (Schlageter)
- Anti-bolshevist operations in the Baltic countries after World War I
- The civil riots (actions of the corps of volunteers) in Germany after World War I
- "White" and "Red" partisan actions during the Russian revolution (especially the campaigns in Siberia: Koltchak)
- Bush war in the Gran-Chaco
- Abyssinian guerrilla operations during the Italian-Abyssinian War
- Republic guerrilla operations during the Spanish Civil War
- Communist Chinese guerrilla operations against the central government and against the Japanese
- Czech exile organization operations during the Second World War
- Activities of the French resistance movement during World War II (Maquis, uprising of the Interior French Forces and the Guerrillas and Partisans)

Operations of the Dutch, Belgian and Norwegian resistance movements during World War II
Activities of the Polish underground movement during the Second World War (Warsaw uprising led by General Bor)
Soviet and Yugoslav partisan operations during World War II
British guerrilla operations behind Japanese lines
Italian partisan operations against the Germans and Neo-Fascists
The start of Werwolf operations in Germany
Communist ELAS-insurrections in Greece after the Second World War
Operations of the illegal Irish Republican Army
Operations of the Algerian and Tunisian resistance movement against the French
Mau-Mau operations in Kenya against the British
North Korean partisan actions against United Nations troops
Resistance movement against the British in Malaya
Vietminh operations against the French (especially during the initial stage)
Anti-Communist riots in East Berlin
Anti-Communist revolution in Hungary
Anti-Communist riots in Poland
EOK-Movement on Cyprus.

Part 1

Organization and Conduct of Guerrilla Warfare

I. Purpose of Guerrilla Warfare

A. General

The purpose of guerrilla warfare is to continue resistance in those parts of the country occupied by the enemy, or to continue the fight after the defeat of the regular army.

Guerrilla detachments cause fear and confusion behind enemy lines; force the enemy to initiate complicated security measures thus wasting his strength; and inflicts losses on both personnel and material.

The entire occupied territory must be pushed into a state of constant unrest so that no invader may move about alone and unarmed.

Service and occupation troops of the enemy will have to take on extra security measures in addition to their numerous other tasks.

The final phase will be a general, open insurrection whose aim will be to force the enemy from the country.

B. Specific targets:

1. Transportation routes (roads and railroad lines)
2. Communications net (telephone lines above and below ground, telephone and radio stations)
3. Power net
4. Vital industrial plants
5. Repair shops and depots
6. Headquarters
7. Transportation convoys
8. Couriers, messengers and liaison officers

C. Characteristics of Guerrilla Warfare

Opposing forces during conventional war are supplied by the factories, warehouses and supply depots; guerrilla units, however, live on the war.

Every guerrilla warfare unit commander has an incomparably larger amount of independence and freedom of action than he would have on the same level of command during a conventional war.

II. Organization of Guerrilla Warfare

1. Formation of Guerrilla Units

Guerrilla units require a nucleus of experienced troops which will serve as instructors and leaders. The enemy tactics of "leaping over" the front by air mobile units or "over-running" the front by armored units will undoubtedly leave many Swiss army units intact. These, in turn, will provide us with a nucleus of trained, experienced fighters for guerrilla units.

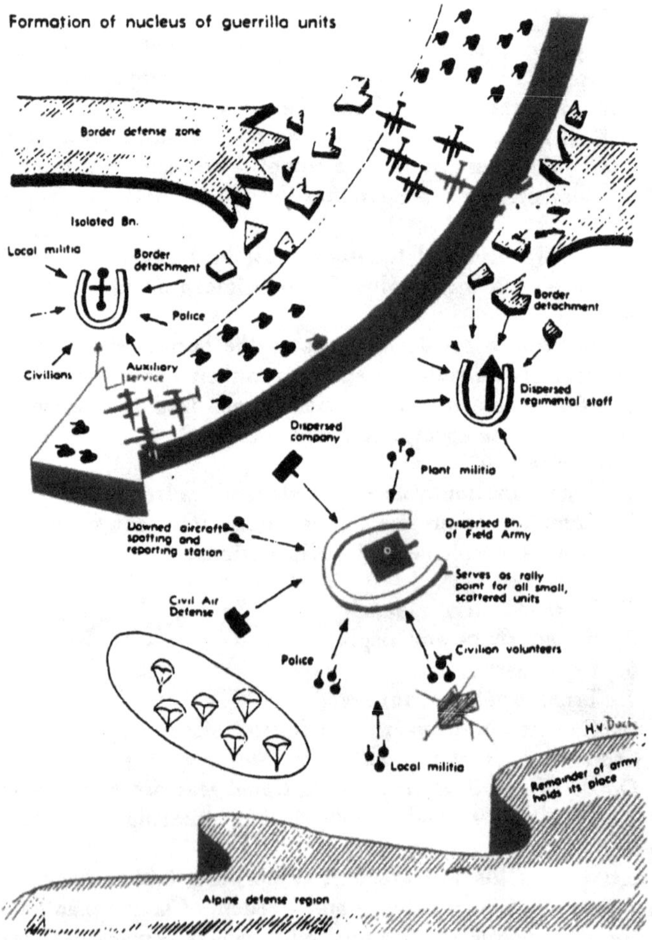

In our army, the majority of the participants in guerrilla warfare will consist of scattered portions of the army or of auxiliary services. It is imperative to bring them together as well as to recruit needed specialists from the civilian population.

Dispersed Batallion or Regimental staffs will rally stragglers as well as combat troops, local militia, auxiliary services, Civil Air Defense personnel, police, and civilian volunteers.

Where no staff personnel are present, alert officers of NCO's will assume command and create an organization.

Higher headquarters—in case such a headquarters still exists and maintains communications—can only issue "general directives" or "operational instructions."

Guerrilla warfare can never be waged near front lines—only on secondary fronts.

Without the support of the civilian population, guerrilla warfare will fail in the long run.

Guerrilla operations will not be initiated near the front lines since the enemy will always be stronger there and the civilian population will be less willing to support GW operations. In addition, enemy regular front line troops normally do not oppress the civilian population. Behind the front, the civilian population, aroused by the terror invoked by political and police organizations which follow the front line troops, will become willing to engage in and support guerrilla operations.

The enemy will hardly commit his strongest fighting units for security and occupation duties or against initial guerrilla operations. Rather, he will utilize second-rate troops which will partially compensate for your weaknesses.

You must distinguish between:

a. Mobile guerrilla units belonging to the army or composed of army elements;
b. Local. stationary elements of the civilian resistance movement.

The idea behind guerrilla warfare is to conduct local resistance operations in the entire occupied territory by the civilian resistance movement (especially sabotage and counter-propaganda). At the same time, it is necessary to create certain liberated areas held by mobile guerrilla units. However, these areas are not to be held rigidly. They will be changed continually in accordance with the foremost rule of guerrilla warfare which states that "no terrain is held permanently."

As a rule, liberated areas can only be held for several weeks or months, until the enemy has concentrated sufficient troops to initiate large-scale counter-guerrilla operations.

By means of continuous small-scale operations conducted by local elements of the civilian resistance movement, you will scatter

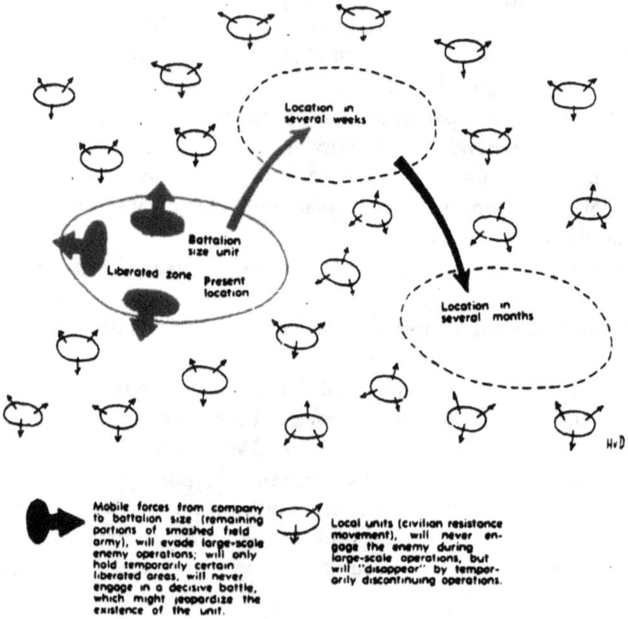

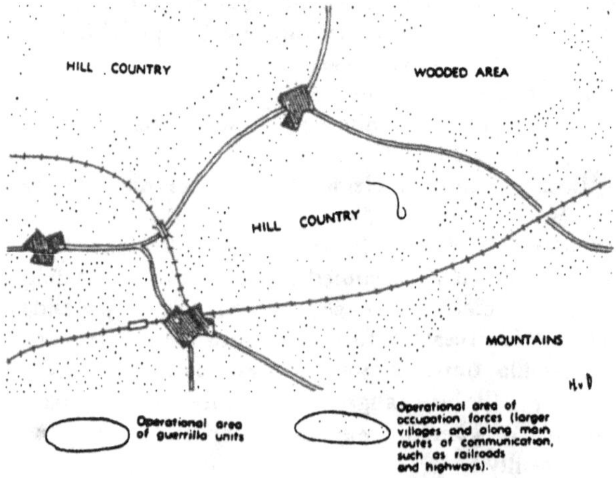

enemy forces, retain the initiative, and protect the organization and development of the mobile guerrilla units.

If you are in a position to form relatively large guerrilla units of approximately battalion size with heavy weapons, the enemy will be unable to occupy firmly the majority of the country, but will

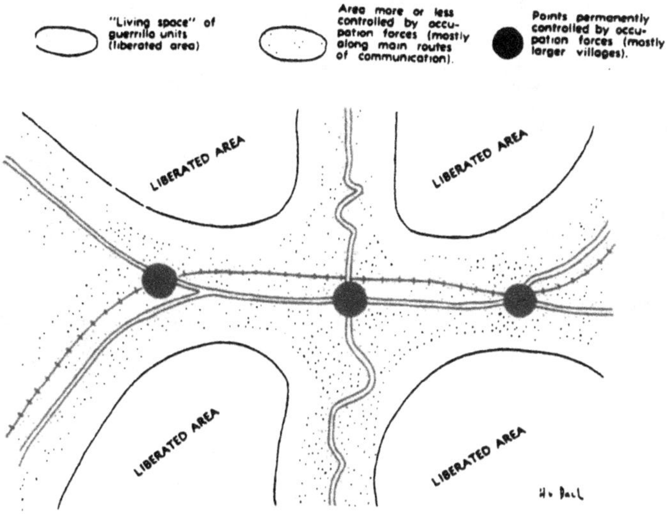

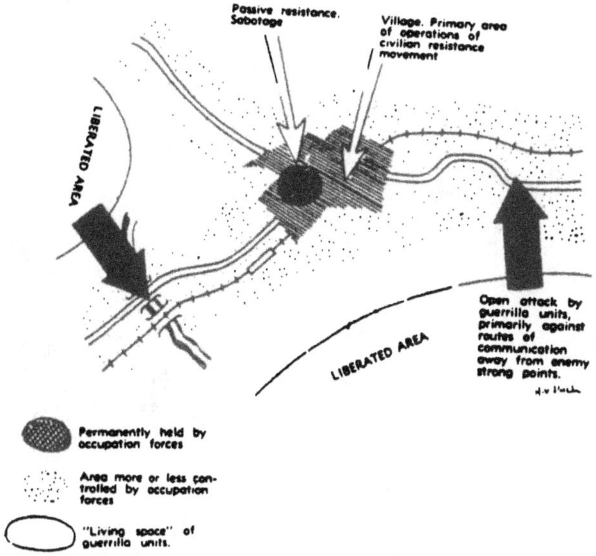

have to be satisfied with controlling key installations and the most important points, primarily routes of transportation and communication.

Ruins in bombed-out cities will also provide good hide-outs. Devastation wrought by atomic weapons will provide excellent places to hide.

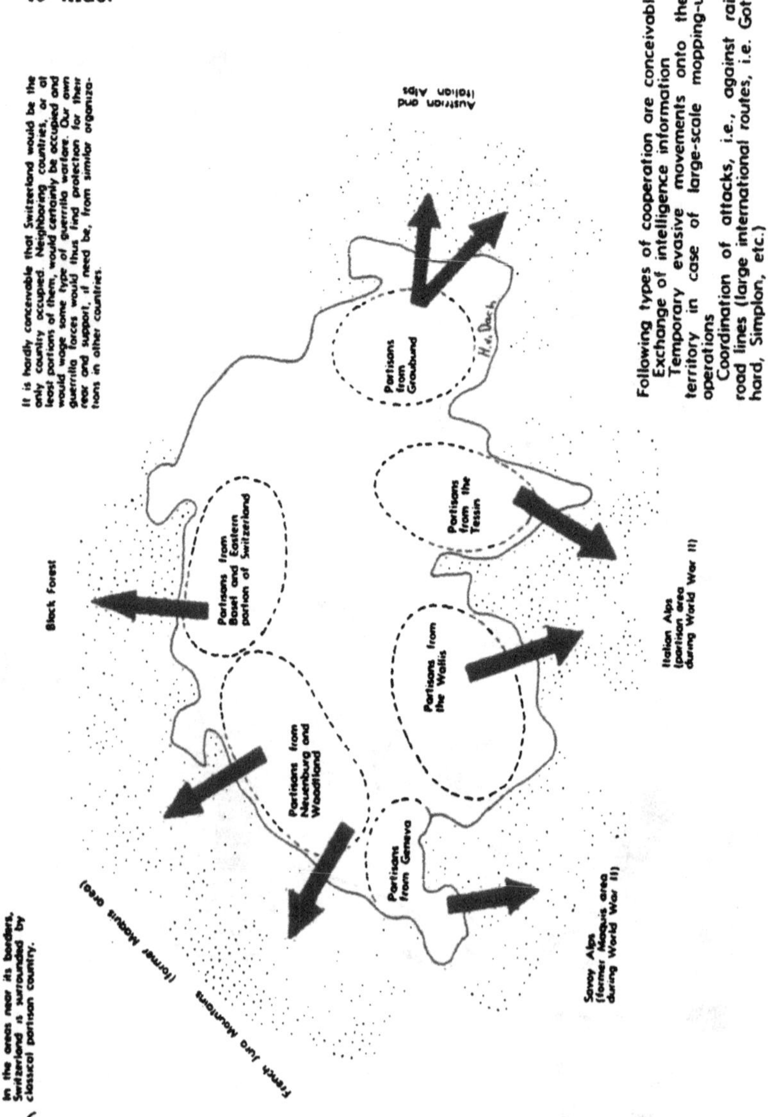

2. Strength of Guerrilla Units

The main problem is to establish a well-balanced ratio of strength among guerrilla units.

When only small guerrilla units are operating, the enemy is able to control occupied territory by means of small, numerous posts containing a squad or a platoon. He will also form a strong central reserve force and install an elaborate net of spies, agents and informers. His control net thus becomes relatively efficient; consequently, the guerrilla unit has little freedom of movement.

However, if you increase guerrilla units from company to battalion size with heavy weapons, the enemy will be forced to create strong garrisons. As a result, he will have to be satisfied with protecting key installations and routes of communication. If he is forced, however, to withdraw all small posts in the intermediate areas and only form a few strong points with reinforced battalions, it will be difficult for him to maintain sufficient reserve forces. Also, agents and informers will be unable to find any support in these areas and can thus be more easily eliminated. The enemy control net becomes thin and your freedom of movement increases.

Guerrilla units of regimental size and above are too cumbersome and easily succumb to the temptation to operate openly in a conventional manner. If they do so, they will easily be destroyed by the superior enemy. Consequently, battalion size units with some heavy infantry weapons (machine guns, mortars) are most appropriate.

Battalion size units are strong enough to attack larger enemy posts successfully (company strong points), yet they are too weak to become tempted to forget the basic rules of guerrilla warfare which are their protection.

From late fall to spring, when no bivouac can be established, unit size will be reduced by dismissing personnel. In summertime, these personnel will be recalled. The same course of action will be followed when food is in short supply.

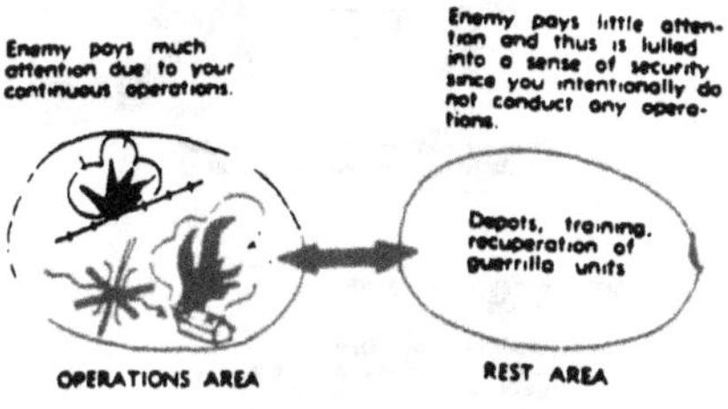

Guerrilla warfare forces the enemy to commit many personnel as guards

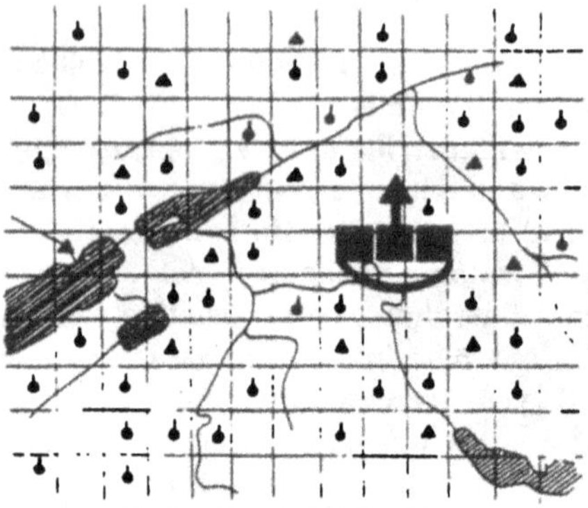

Small guerrilla units will permit the enemy to commit small occupation detachments. Small occupation detachments permit the establishment of many individual posts. Many posts result in a dense observation and control net. Such a net will restrict the operations of our guerrilla units. Agents and informers will find support and help everywhere in the intermediate zone. The enemy will be able to establish a strong central reserve force.

Situation with small guerrilla units (Squads and Platoons)

Legend:

Police post from squad to maximum of platoon

Strong point, company size at most

Central reserves (mechanized police regiment) used as "counter-attack reserve" against local riots and insubordination

Efficient agent and informer net

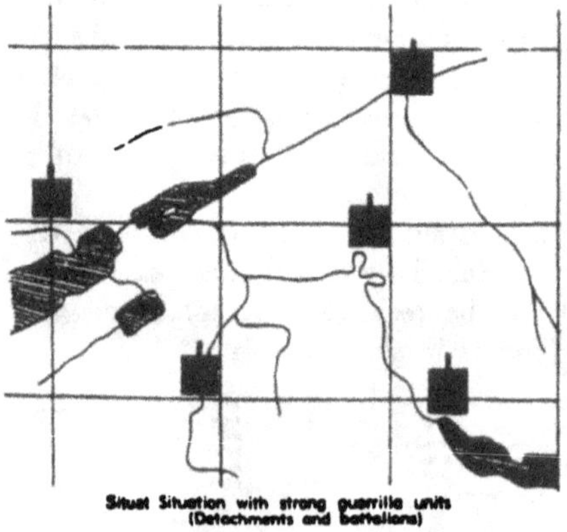

Strong guerrilla units with heavy weapons force the enemy to establish large strong points. With the forces available the enemy will only be able to establish a few such strong points. Fewer posts will result in a less efficient control and observation net. You thus have greater freedom of movement. Agents and informers will be unable to find support in the intermediate area and can be easily eliminated. It will be difficult for the enemy to establish a strong central reserve force.

Situat Situation with strong guerrilla units (Detachments and battalions)

Legend:

Large enemy strong point—Battalion size

Enemy must withdraw from all small posts in the intermediate area or they will be easily destroyed by your guerrilla units.

3. Replacements for Guerrilla Headquarters

In order to wage an effective guerrilla war, headquarter units will need a variety of trained personnel. If need be, these personnel can be recruited from the civilian population.

Postal, telephone, and telegraph employees as well as railroad employees and power technicians can provide technical advice for sabotage operations.

Radio technicians can organize communication nets between guerrilla units and the remainder of the army holding out in a rear area, the civilian resistance movement and friendly foreign countries (if our own army headquarters no longer exists).

Engineer officers will serve as demolition specialists.

Prominent politicians, newspaper editors, etc., can serve as liaison personnel between guerrilla units and the local populace, and the civilian resistance movement.

Editors and other newspaper personnel will operate guerrilla controlled presses in cooperation with the civilian resistance movement.

A list of the above mentioned technicians will be kept by the personnel section at headquarters.

4. Organizational Phase

The enemy will leave certain areas unoccupied due to their lack of importance. He will be unable to occupy some areas because of insufficient personnel.

You have to move into all of these areas.

Assemble small groups of personnel at these places. Remain inactive until your group is well organized.

You must not provoke the enemy into taking counter measures against you during your moment of greatest vulnerability, i.e., during phases of organization and initial activation. Never again, not even in the most critical situations when pursued or even encircled, will your unit be as vulnerable and as in danger of disintegrating as it is during this initial phase.

Shortage of trained personnel or technicians can be compensated for by recruiting suitable personnel from among the civilian population. By the same means, you will later replace personnel losses. Every civilian who joins you is permanently removed from enemy terrorist actions—arrest of entire clans, deportation, execution of hostages, etc.

Organizational tasks:

Chief of Future
Guerrilla Unit

Population

Find out who is generally reliable. Find out who is willing to help passively, i.e., supply food. provide intelligence information, etc. Find out who is willing to help actively, i.e., laying mines, serving as guides, hiding and caring for the wounded and sick. Find out who is passively supporting the enemy, i.e., followers, profiteers. Determine who actively works with the enemy.

Guerrilla Unit

Organize combat units (squads, platoons). Procure ammunition. Procure food. Obtain equipment (clothes, shoes, rucksacks, etc.). Stockpile arms. Train personnel with captured weapons. Convert artillery personnel into mortar personnel. Convert auxiliary personnel, police, civil air defense personnel, members of supply and postal units into make-shift "infantry personnel."

Even with experienced soldiers it is still necessary to implement a short training period. This serves: a. to acquaint leaders with their new personnel: b. to allow personnel to become familiar with one another. Training also familiarizes personnel with the basic tactics and techniques of guerrilla warfare such as march, security, liaison, communications, reconnaissance, techniques of sabotage and demolition; with the use of captured weapons and ammunition such as hand grenades, mines, explosives, etc.

This training will take up to one or two months, depending upon whether you are already being pursued or still organizing unmolested, or whether operations have to be conducted immediately.

The longer the organization phase the greater the chances of success as there will be fewer losses during future engagements. This in turn will increase self-confidence.

Reconnaissance of future targets and systematic observation of the enemy can be carried on concurrently with organization and training.

Members of engineer and demolition units as well as infantry personnel and combat patrol experts will be incorporated into your guerrilla unit. However, since they will only account for a small percentage of your personnel it will be necessary to train other individuals in these fields.

Artillery personnel will be converted into mortar personnel.

Members of light motorized units; tank crews, drivers; pilots, ground personnel; anti-aircraft personnel, air defense personnel; postal and supply personnel; police, local militia, auxiliary service personnel will be utilized as infantry.

Civilian volunteers will be drawn from the following sources:

a. Individuals under draft age—cadets, pathfinders, pre-military trainees, and rifle club members.

b. Individuals who have completed their obligatory military service.

c. Individuals formerly found unfit for military service or those discharged for medical reasons.

d. Individuals exempted from service who worked for institutions essential to the war effort but which are now under enemy control such as railroad and postal employees, etc.

Recruit amateur radio operators for replacements for operators. If necessary, obtain them through the civilian resistance movement.

Assign chaplains and civilian priests to the medical section. They are well suited as liasion personnel with the population, especially in the country. They can maintain contact with wounded guerrillas whom you have left with the population to be cared for "undercover."

Use armorers, and perhaps, civilian mechanics as instructors on captured weapons. Since they will quickly learn the operation of foreign weapons due to their technical background, they can instruct other personnel in their operation.

5. Leadership

Select leaders carefully. Guerrilla personnel must respect and accept their leader. Once behind enemy lines, no military policeman, no military court, nor any state power will help the guerrilla leader maintain discipline and fighting spirit. Military rank will then only play a subordinate role.

An individual who leads by "bluff" is not suitable. He may be able to maintain his position in a conventional unit for some time due to the chain of command and discipline, but never in a guerrilla unit.

Only real "troop leaders" who know how to handle people can maintain their position.

The leader must also possess some technical knowledge since during guerrilla warfare it is less important to make great "leader-

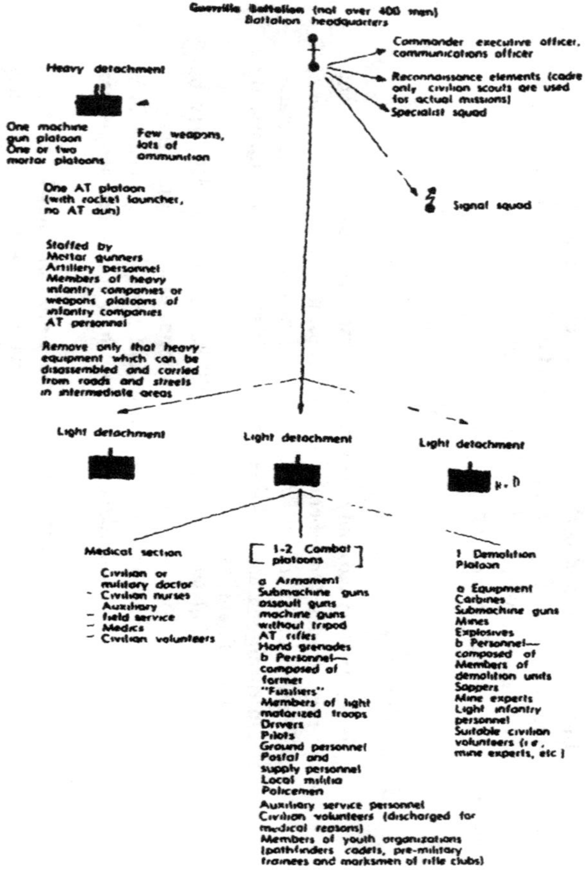

Guerrilla Battalion (not over 400 men)
Battalion headquarters
Commander executive officer, communications officer
Reconnaissance elements (cadre only, civilian scouts are used for actual missions)
Specialist squad
Signal squad
Heavy detachment
One machine gun platoon
One or two mortar platoons
Few weapons, lots of ammunition
One AT platoon (with rocket launcher, no AT gun)
Staffed by
Mortar gunners
Artillery personnel
Members of heavy infantry companies or weapons platoons of infantry companies
AT personnel
Remove only that heavy equipment which can be disassembled and carried from roads and streets in intermediate areas
Light detachment
Light detachment
Light detachment
Medical section
Civilian or military doctor
- Civilian nurses
Auxiliary
- field service
- Medics
- Civilian volunteers
1-2 Combat platoons
a Armament
Submachine guns
assault guns
machine guns without tripod
AT rifles
Hand grenades
b Personnel—composed of
former "Fusiliers"
Members of light motorized troops
Drivers
Pilots
Ground personnel
Postal and supply personnel
Local militia
Policemen
Auxiliary service personnel
Civilian volunteers (discharged for medical reasons)
Members of youth organizations (pathfinders cadets, pre-military trainees and marksmen of rifle clubs)
1 Demolition Platoon
a Equipment
Carbines
Submachine guns
Mines
Explosives
b Personnel—composed of
Members of demolition units
Sappers
Mine experts
Light infantry personnel
Suitable civilian volunteers (i.e., mine experts, etc.)

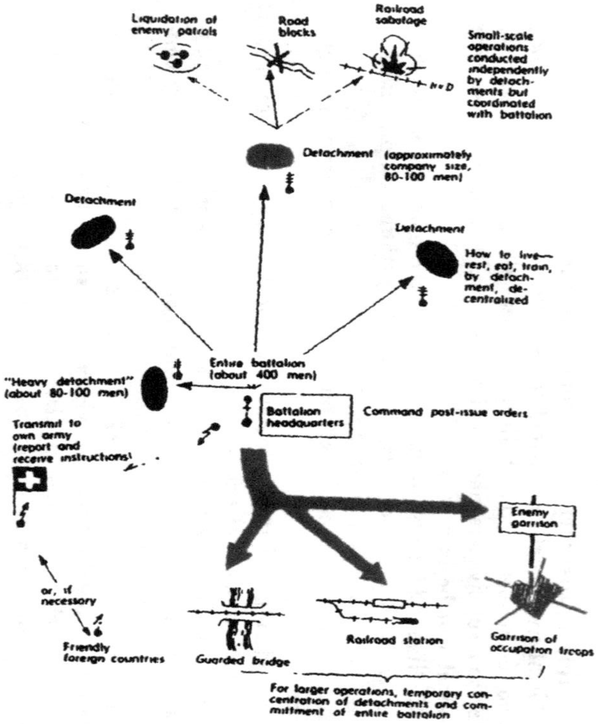

Liquidation of enemy patrols
Road blocks
Railroad sabotage
Small-scale operations conducted independently by detachments but coordinated with battalion
Detachment (approximately company size, 80-100 men)
Detachment
Detachment
How to live—rest, eat, train, by detachment, decentralized
Entire battalion (about 400 men)
"Heavy detachment" (about 80-100 men)
Battalion headquarters
Command post-issue orders
Transmit to own army (report and receive instructions)
or, if necessary
Friendly foreign countries
Guarded bridge
Railroad station
Enemy garrison
Garrison of occupation troops
For larger operations, temporary concentration of detachments and commitment of entire battalion

ship decisions" than to conduct efficiently some relatively simple operations with finesse. He should be well versed in small unit tactics as well as mine and demolition techniques.

6. Equipment

Since a considerable percentage of your people will consist of auxiliary service personnel, local militia, plant militia, police and civilian volunteers, you will lack many items of individual clothing, from shelter halves and suitable shoes to canteens and thermos bottles.

Obtain some sort of "field uniform," i.e., outer clothing, overalls, ski suits or jackets, windbreakers, etc.

Items of personal equipment, such as knife, fork, and spoon, mess kit, small cooking stoves, flashlights, rucksacks, etc., can be procured; by stripping these items from each dead enemy, by soliciting said items from the population, from shops in larger towns by members of the civilian resistance movement.

Procure tents from civilian sporting goods stores or from outdoorsmen with whom your men are acquainted.

Guerrillas dressed in civilian clothes can collect these items, or have them brought to you by members of the resistance movement.

Make preparations for winter as early as possible. These include the procurement of blankets, good shoes, and protective clothing such as overcoats, windbreakers, ski jackets, warm under garments. Trusted women can tailor make-shift snow suits made out of bed sheets.

Procure two radios per detachment—one for use on a power net and one portable set with batteries for reception in lonely regions where no power net is available (mountains, forests).

Build up the supply of batteries for your portable radios with help of the resistance movement. Secure and hide these early since the enemy will soon requisition all radios and accessories from the population.

Have your "amateur radio operators" operate your radios. They are technically skilled and can perform repairs with limited means.

With these radios you will be able to monitor enemy broadcasts as well as those from friendly foreign countries and your own exile government.

By equipping each guerrilla detachment and each radio of the civilian resistance movement with ordinary radios, it will be possible for your own army headquarters in the safe area, and your exile government abroad to communicate with you. They can communicate over long distances providing advice and technical guidance for guerrilla operations or indicating specific targets which you are to attack. Furthermore, your morale and ability to resist will increase since you will feel less lonely and lost.

7. Supply of Weapons

Usually it will be easier to obtain weapons than ammunition. Crew-served weapons—submachine guns, light machine guns, heavy machine guns, rocket launchers, mortars—will come from dispersed elements of the regular army. These elements will provide the nucleus of your battalion firepower.

Auxiliary service personnel, local militia and police will, as a rule, be able to bring their individual weapons—pistols, carbines, submachine guns.

Supplying civilian volunteers with weapons will pose the greatest problem. Below are several ways you may solve this problem:

a. Collect weapons from poorly policed battlefields. Remove usable weapons from destroyed tanks, fortifications, and downed airplanes.

b. Remove weapons from the dead enemy.

c. In practically all Swiss families, you will find an older, but usable, weapon (rifle 11, carbine 35).

d. Collect privately owned weapons of hunters and marksmen. The owners will donate their weapons willingly because they run the risk of execution if the enemy finds they have concealed them.

e. Requisition weapons from civilian arms shops or police stations which eventually would have to surrender their weapons to the enemy.

8. Supply of Ammunition and Explosives

a. Basic sources of supply:

(1) Ammunition which dispersed army units have with them
(2) Ammunition supplied from hidden caches established according to plan by the retreating army
(3) Ammunition systematically stripped from each enemy casualty
(4) Ammunition collected in raids on enemy transport and depots

(5) Ammunition collected from poorly policed battlefields—from destroyed tanks, field fortifications, downed planes, etc.

(6) Explosives retrieved by removal of mines from partially cleared or uncleared mine fields

b. Possible sources of supply:

(1) Sporadic air drops from a rear stronghold

(2) Systematic air drops from friendly foreign countries

Collecting weapons and ammunition from private parties such as hunters, marksmen, police stations, civilian rifle clubs. Requisition explosives and detonators from civilian construction companies and quarries, farmers and lumber jacks.

Requisition all air rifles and ammunition from farmers. Such weapons are especially suitable for "special operations," such as attacking individuals without making noise. If possible, procure two to three air rifles and pistols per detachment.

Construct a camouflaged ammunition cache. Humidity is the greatest enemy of ammunition; therefore the cache must be carefully constructed. Build a grate using boards and logs, so that the packages will not lie on the ground.

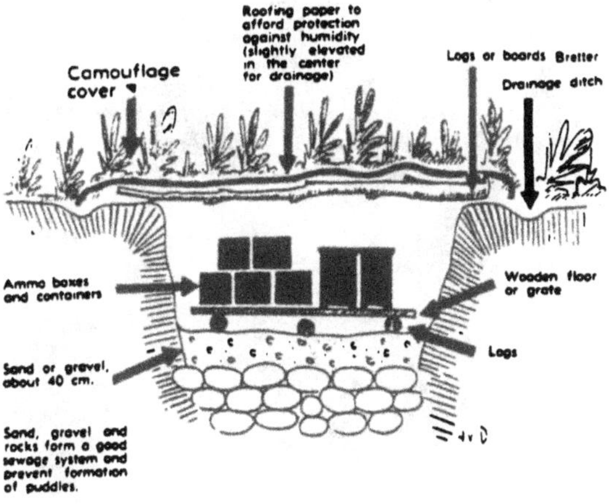

Leave an interval of about the width of a hand between boxes and containers to afford air circulation. Insert roof lath between rows to provide for air circulation. Air the depot by removing the roofing paper as often as possible.

Homemade Grenades

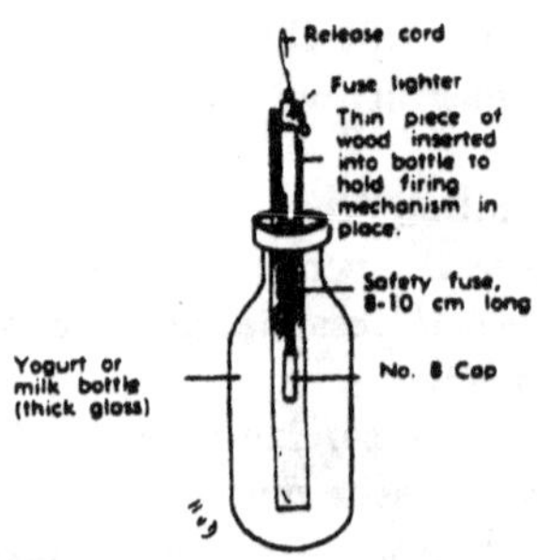

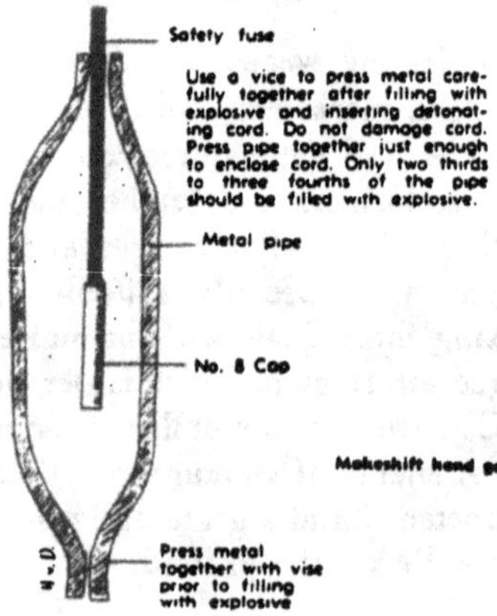

Makeshift hand grenade

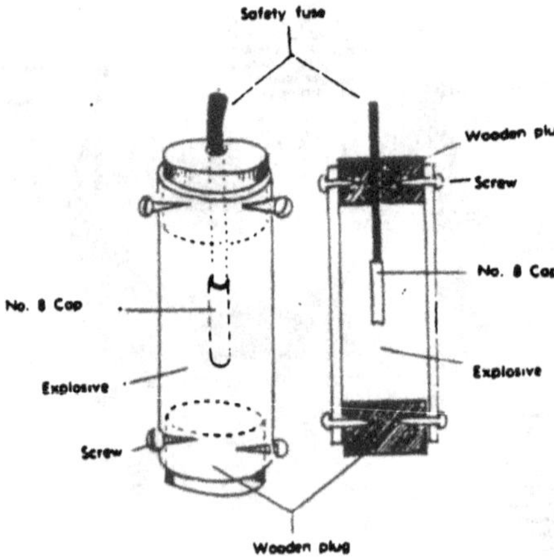

Improvised, concentrated charges can be used to destroy fixed objects (railroad tracks, power line poles, transformers, etc.).

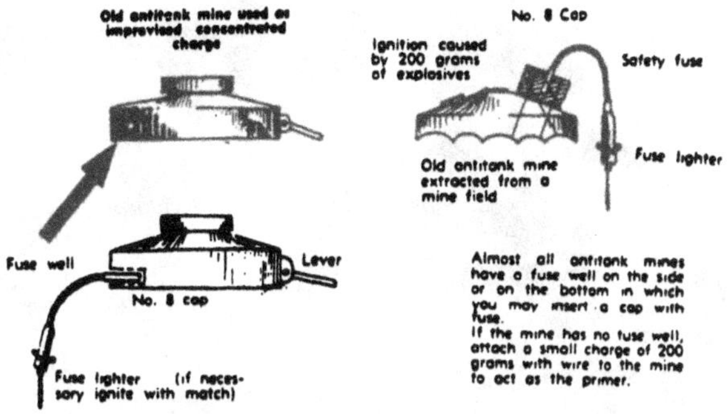

Antitank mines serve as excellent, improvised, concentrated charges. Weight of explosive contained is always three to four kilograms.

Artillery projectiles, mortar rounds and aerial bombs can be used as improvised, concentrated charges to destroy hard targets.

It is best to attach the projectile to a board with wire. For a primer, use a small charge which is always attached near the detonator of the projectile.

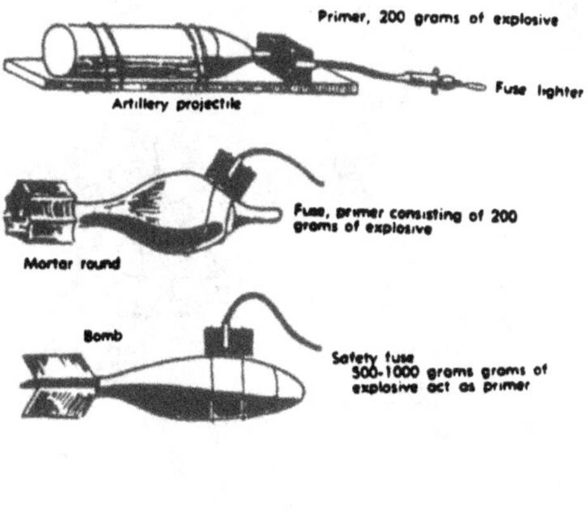

Makeshift hand grenades made of yogurt glasses (200-300 grams of explosive). Effective radius: 4 to 5 meters. The glass will not break upon impact except on concrete roads.

Makeshift charge in can (1 to 1.5 kg of explosive). Effective radius: 15 to 20 meters.

At left, ignite with match or cigarette.

At right, ignite by means of fuse lighter.

Ignite either with match, cigarette or fuselighter (in photo a fuse-lighter is used).

Increase fragmentation effect by adding stones, and pieces of scrap metal or nails.

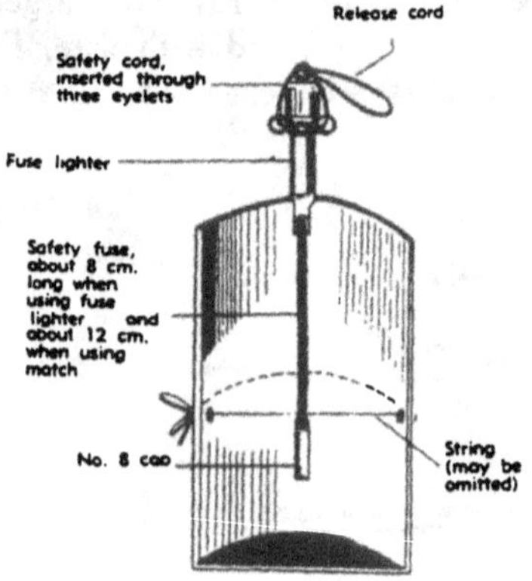

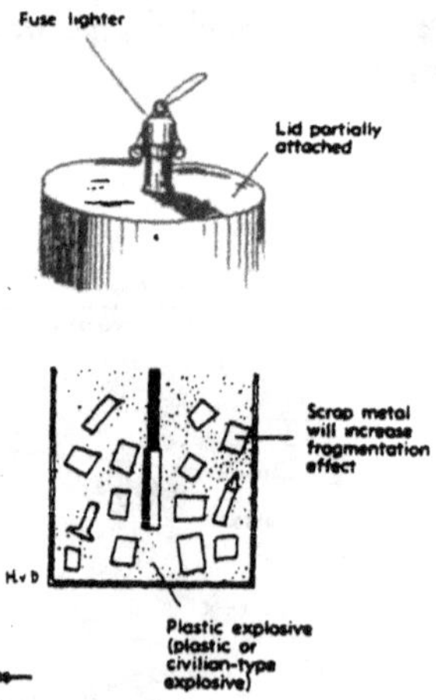

Anti-personnel grenades—throw into marching columns, billets, offices, etc.

9. Organization of Maintenance Facilities

Distinguish between repair shops in "liberated areas" and repair shops in "occupied areas." Install make-shift ordinance shops in civilian locksmith shops, blacksmith shops, and garages.

Your maintenance personnel, disguised in civilian clothes, can perform repairs in these shops which cannot be done in the field.

10. Organization of Food Supply

Guerrilla units ordinarily live off the land as well as from material taken from the enemy. Occasionally they establish depots.

In "liberated areas," i.e., in those areas over which guerrilla units have temporary control, food supplies are requisitioned from farmers, mills, shops and perhaps warehouses. It is obvious in such situations that friction may very easily arise between the population and guerrilla units. In this case, the "liaison man" to the population (see replacements for guerrilla headquarters) has to act along with the detachment commander to reduce the possibility of alienating the populace. (See section on "Relationship with population.")

The question of food supply, a difficult one to solve, has considerable bearing upon the tactics of guerrilla units.

As a result, detachments (approximately one company) live alone and battalions are only formed for larger operations. It is easier to feed scattered detachments of 80 to 100 men each off the land than it would be in the case of a 400-man battalion.

If you have high-grade and non-perishable food supplies or have captured those, keep them for the difficult times in winter. High-grade food items are canned milk, chocolate, ovomaltine, crackers, canned items containing lots of oil and fat, smoked meat, bacon and hard sausages. It is advisable to store these items in well hidden depots.

Food supply suggestions: When supplied by the population, be careful not to expose yourself any longer than necessary. In summertime, send out personnel in advance to have the population prepare the food. Then have it picked up by a "pick-up team" and eat in the open as you are safer there than in a village. In wintertime, wait under cover and only come to the houses to eat in a warm place when the food is actually ready. Obviously, these strict security measures can be relaxed—especially in wintertime—when operating in a liberated area.

11. Organization of Medical Service and Procurement of Medical Supplies

Do not establish an elaborate medical service. The operation of field hospitals will be impossible, since units are constantly moving in a liberated area and often move from one liberated area to another.

Provide only first aid. Take wounded and sick personnel to reliable persons among the population who will hide and care for them.

Doctors and medics with medical supplies and equipment are indispensable for guerrilla units and must be recruited from among the civilian population.

Medical Supplies.

a. Sources:
   (1) Supplies still in possession of dispersed army units
   (2) Supplies taken from the enemy

b. Procurement—with assistance of the civilian resistance movement—from:
   (1) Civilian doctors
   (2) Civilian pharmacies and drugstores
   (3) Civilian hospitals
   (4) Aid stations in large industrial plans
   (5) Private homes (systematically scrounge small quantities)
   (6) Pharmaceutical industries (surreptitious delivery by civilian resistance movement)

12. Relationship with the Population

The population is your greatest friend. Without their sympathy and active support you will be unable to exist for extended periods of time. As a result, you can ill afford to alienate them by brutal behavior or lack of discipline. Such provacation should never happen. The possibility exists that guerrilla units may become a greater evil than the occupation forces.

If you have to requisition something, do not demand it with a submachine gun, but appeal to the common goal and patriotism.

Do not forget that the laws of the conventional war hardly apply any more; each old man, each woman and each child can harm you greatly if they want to. For better or worse, you are practically dependent upon the good will of the population. You also depend upon their steady, "I do not know, I have not heard nor seen anything," replies to enemy interrogators, even when this attitude might mean their deportation and death.

Initially, the population will be intimidated and without courage. This will change, however, with a longer war and occupation.

An awakened, aroused population can support you in many ways.

Passive support:

a. Observe the enemy systematically and continuously
b. Establish an inconspicuous security net for guerrilla units
c. Procure supplies
d. Hide and care for wounded and sick
e. Conceal material and ammunition
f. Serve as guides for guerrilla units
g. Identify collaborators

Active support:

a. Supply technicians for guerrilla units
b. Replace wounded and killed personnel
c. Lay mines
d. Sabotage wire communications

Even if the population should act only half-heartedly in your behalf, you will always find some people willing to help you as observers, scouts, and messengers.

As chief of the guerrilla detachment, you must be extremely cautious in your contact with elements of the civilian resistance movement, even in liberated areas. Don't forget that you have to change positions rapidly. Members of the resistance movement, however, are locally restricted and have to continue operations according to your directives. Consequently, you must not expose their "cover" for the sake of temporary advantages, or else they will be captured and liquidated by the enemy after your departure.

III. Tactics of Guerrilla Units

1. Your First Guerrilla Operations

For your first objectives, select simple targets which you can master without any major difficulties such as demolition of high tension power poles, or laying mines on throughfares.

Only after certain *esprit de corps* has been established in your unit and after the self-confidence of your people has risen because of a few successful operations, are you in a position to undertake larger operations—operations against railroad stations, bridges; ambushing marching columns, etc.

You will quite necessarily suffer losses and setbacks. However, your unit will have become sufficiently stable in the meantime to be able to withstand reverses without falling apart.

As a leader you must get used to the fact that during guerrilla warfare many more, and sometimes entirely different, psychological factors have to be taken into consideration than in the regular army. Here you were always suported—perhaps without your realizing it—by the ever-present power of the state (laws, courts, police) to maintain discipline.

Schematic acceleration of operations:

Raids on individual soldiers
Raids on small guard posts
Raids on individual patrols ← Results in captured ammunition and weapons
Raids on small columns

Results in captured ammunition and weapons
↓
You thus gain tactical control of "No Man's Land"

Raids on small columns
↓
Ambushes, raids, suprise attacks
↓
You thus interrupt or endanger communication between individual enemy detachments
→
You occasionally capture heavy weapons
↓
Heavy weapons enable you to attack fixed strong points; first small ones, then larger ones.
↓
Your attacks will force the occupation troops to withdraw from all smaller strong points and outposts. Consequently, both no-man's-land and the individual liberated areas grow larger. Periodically, the enemy will, however, recover and attempt to deal heavy blows against you which you must evade.

2. (Operational) Security of Guerrilla Units

The security of guerrilla units will generally be carried out by the civilian resistance movement through:

a. Espionage

(1) Systematically sound out occupation personnel

(2) Report carelessly made remarks

(3) Monitor radio and telephone conversations

(4) Bribe officials of the occupation forces

(5) Blackmail officials of the occupation forces

b. Observation

(1) Constantly observe roads, railroads, railroad stations, and airports, in order to detect the assembly of airborne or helicopter units as well as the approach of motorized columns and railroad transports.

(2) The civilian resistance movement can report results of reconnaissance missions by radio, messengers, or carrier pigeons. Either members of the resistance movement or, preferably, liaison personnel of the guerrilla units attached to the headquarters of the local resistance movement can serve as messengers.

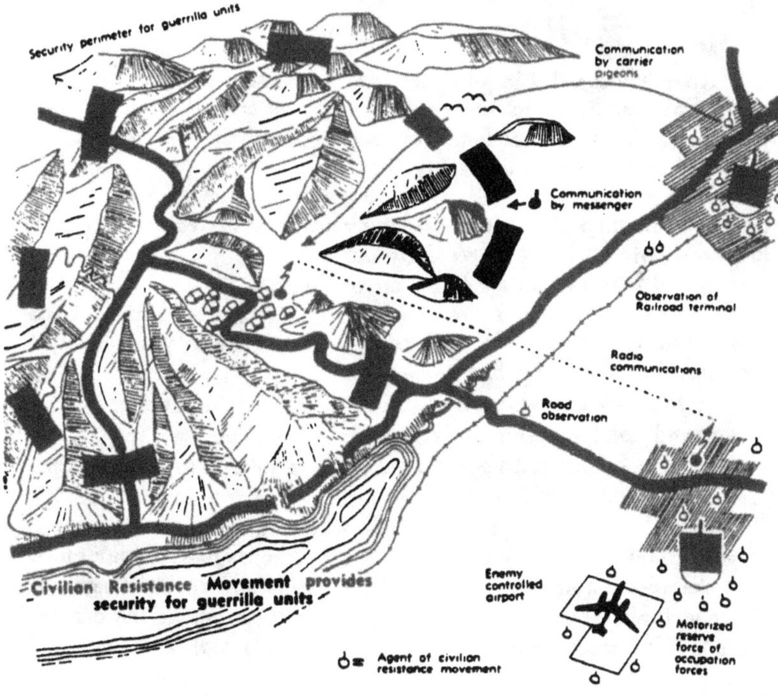

3. General Behavior

a. Proceed with secrecy, care, and cunning—even with slyness.
b. Only use force when you can mass superior forces.
c. Avoid any fight which might jeopardize the existence of your unit.
d. The most important thing for your safety is maintaining secrecy.
e. Ambushes and raids are your main fighting weapons.
f. Never engage a strong enemy and never accept an open fight.
g. When meeting a superior enemy you must divide into small groups, avoid the enemy and reassemble later at pre-designated rally points.

If you cannot avoid a fight with pursuing troops, do not engage in a decisive fight under any circumstances. Rather adopt delaying actions and break contact with the enemy as quickly as possible—certainly no later than nighttime which will conceal your movements.

Once the occupation troops have gained relief by means of a successful attack and returned to their strong points, harrass them again. Guerrilla units should reappear from hiding once the enemy columns have disappeared.

4. March

After a successful large operation you must move to a new area of operations. Prior to movement, establish contact with reliable persons in the new area. Send out one or two NCO's in advance to reconnoitre the area thoroughly.

You as the commander will roughly outline the route to be taken on the map and then consider by what means you will change locations without being detected by the enemy.

Avoid highways and villages on the march.

No long preparations or preparatory orders should give notice of impending change. You must keep your decision to yourself until the time for movement has come.

If you have to make extensive preparations (i.e., moving ammunition and food supplies or large-scale reconnaissance), try to devise a cover by circulating a rumor about a false plan which seems credible and does not arouse suspicion.

In order to intercept individuals who might inform the enemy of your plans, send out several patrols a few hours before your move in order to lay ambushes far ahead on streets and roads. They will apprehend all persons passing by and detain them during the critical period. If necessary, cut telephone communications also.

Whenever you encounter unfamiliar terrain, obtain scouts familiar with the area. However, release them only when they cannot possibly compromise your operations.

Nobody should be allowed to know where you come from or where you are going. Your next operational area must be kept secret from everyone.

Deceive the population about your strength. Always create the impression of being stronger than you really are (i.e., the remark: ". . . we are only the advance guard of a larger unit which follows over there").

If possible, only travel during the night in order to minimize possibility of your position being compromised.

Since you have to avoid roads, the method of travel will usually be by foot. Obviously, you will have to march a lot. However, do not require unnecessary forced marches. Keep your men fresh and conserve their strength so that they will be in shape for any operation or movement.

If possible always march in a closed formation. When everybody is close together, quick decisions can be made and implemented better and faster.

Provide front and rear security by sending three to four men several hundred meters ahead and to the rear of your formation.

5. Rest

Move at night and rest in the woods during the day.

Select woods for shelter. When forced to camp out in the open, utilize high points which will provide good observation.

Security elements placed too far forward only endanger you. While resting, security is best established by placing guards in the

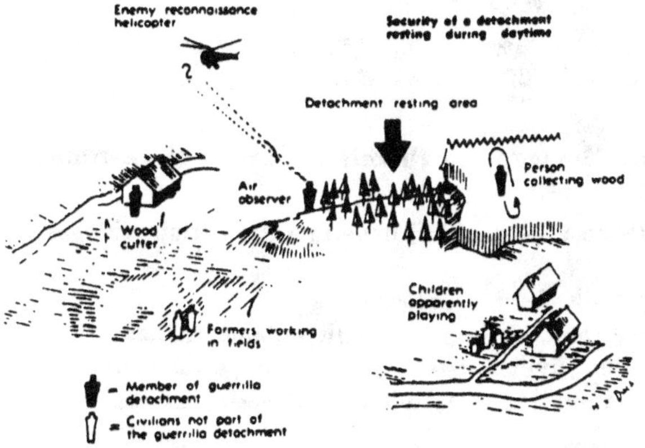

immediate vicinity of the camp. Also, enlist civilians for this purpose as they can observe the enemy in an inconspicuous manner.

Post air observers during daytime at your resting places. At night, you will place two-man ambushes on each likely avenue of approach.

If you bivouac after nightfall, keep the detachment together and post several two-man guard posts at 50 or at the most 100 meters from the detachment. As visibility increases after dawn you must increase security.

To preclude being surprised by air mobile units which are your greatest enemy, be sure to designate guards to scan the skies.

Never use the same camp two nights in a row, unless you are in a "liberated area." Never spend the night in the same place where you have rested during the day.

Issue new alert instructions every day so that everyone will know what to do in case of a raid. At the same time designate a rally point for stragglers.

Personnel detailed elsewhere (individuals or entire units) must be kept informed of the location of rally points where they can join you later or least find out where the detachment has moved to.

Security of a detachment at night

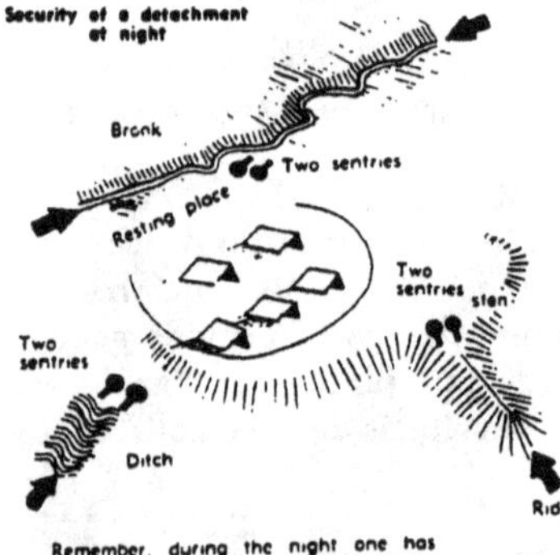

Remember, during the night one has the tendency to follow natural terrain features while in the approach. It is here that you must post your sentry team

6. Relay Simple Messages by Primitive Means of Communications

a. From time to time you will have to enter certain villages in order to:

(1) Replenish food supplies
(2) Leave wounded and sick with reliable civilians
(3) Use the civilian telephone or the postal system (see section on "Use of telephone and postal service.")

b. Simple messages can be relayed to you by civilians (mostly members of the resistance movement) by:

(1) Opening or closing of pre-designated windows or shutters

(2) Hanging out clothes

(3) Displaying or concealing carriages, etc.

Smoke and light signals as well as waving of sheets are too obvious and too dangerous for the signaller. It is best to refrain from such signalling.

With these primitive, yet inconspicuous means, only very simple messages can be relayed, such as:

"Attention, danger! Enemy in village!" or

"No danger! Village free of enemy!"

Use the above mentioned signals in such a way that they can be recognized with binoculars from the edge of nearby woods.

7. Construction of Road Blocks

Felled or blasted trees are best suited for road blocks. Do not drop to big a tree in hopes of causing the enemy more work. You only waste a lot of time and explosive.

If you do not have the means of installing booby traps with your road blocks, at least simulate them. Below are some examples:

Separate, half hidden wires leading from tree branches into the ground which simulate trip wires to hidden charges.

Loose and only partially covered pieces of sod next to the road (enemy may assume that poorly concealed mines are placed here).

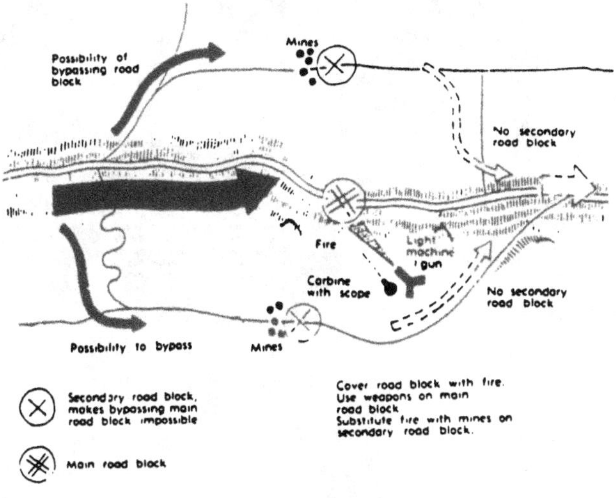

In guerrilla warfare you must install road blocks on open roads, where the enemy must expose himself to fire while removing them. This, of course, is contrary to everything you have learned about the construction of road blocks for a conventional war. However, you must learn to think differently for guerrilla warfare.

With smaller trees you will need little explosives or will need little time to expose yourself to enemy patrols while cutting them.

Booby traps on improvised road blocks are the most important thing and not trees as such.

The enemy will not remove the trees by hand but will haul them away by vehicle. However, when booby traps are attached he will need an armored vehicle, either a tank or armored personnel carrier, in order to be able to clear the road immediately and without regard to any possible explosions, or he has to get specialists (Engineers) to search for the booby traps and disarm them. In any case this will cause a loss of time.

If the enemy is so ruthless that personnel losses caused by mines are of no consequence and he commits everybody—even untrained personnel—to remove booby traps, the enemy will suffer casualties and you will have achieved your goal.

Sabotage on roads is less effective than sabotage on railroads since each road block may be easily bypassed by rerouting traffic.

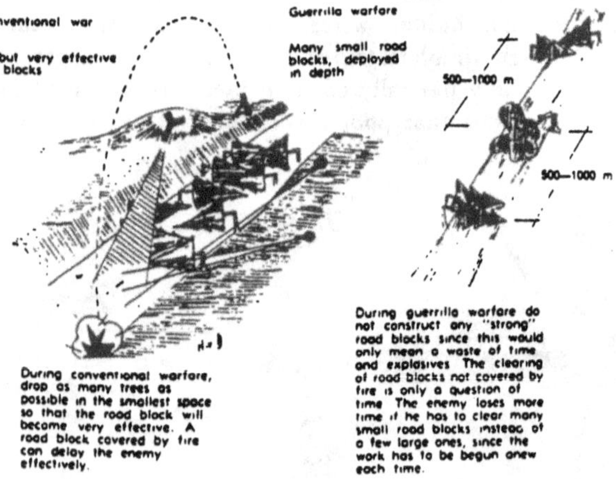

During conventional warfare, drop as many trees as possible in the smallest space so that the road block will become very effective. A road block covered by fire can delay the enemy effectively.

During guerrilla warfare do not construct any "strong" road blocks since this would only mean a waste of time and explosives The clearing of road blocks not covered by fire is only a question of time The enemy loses more time if he has to clear many small road blocks instead of a few large ones, since the work has to be begun anew each time.

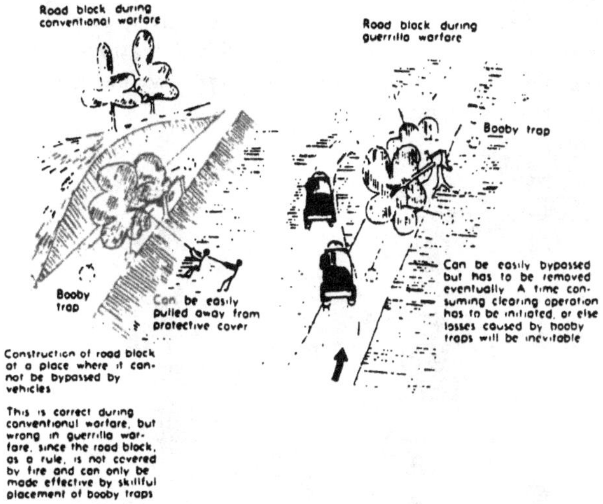

8. Mining of Roads

With stake mines	Advantage:	Quickly emplaced.
	Disadvantage:	Dangerous to own population since little tension required to set it off.
Uncontrolled mine 49	Advantage:	No danger to the population as mine can be only detonated by heavy vehicles—trucks, tanks, etc.
	Disadvantage:	Much time required while laying. Placement takes about 10 minutes per mine during which you may be surprised by enemy patrols.
Uncontrolled mine 37	Disadvantage:	Much time required as for mine 49; in addition, it is dangerous to population—it can be set off by little pressure.

9. Sabotage of Road Net

Destroy, change or remove road signs.

Place nails on road. Only effective when used in large quantities. The population should be used in this type operation. The enemy will be forced to embark on a systematic road clearing operation (they may impress the local populace to help them). At any rate, sabotage operations of this nature will cause the enemy a great loss of time. Coordination of this type of sabotage with operations at the front is indispensable since such sabotage is only of value when the enemy has to use roads continually.

Sabotage of Vehicles

How can you sabotage a motor vehicle in such a manner that the breakdown will not be detected immediately but will require complicated and time consuming repairs?

a. Sugar in gas tank
b. Water in gas tank
c. Loosen oil drainage screw to cause loss of oil
d. Loosen screw on oil filter
e. Loosen oil pressure lead

How can you mistreat a motor vehicle so that is is disabled quickly without revealing that you committed sabotage?

a. Fill battery with plain water (destroy battery)
b. Grease partially or not at all (wear-out bearings)
c. Do not fill with sufficient oil (will burn out bearings)
d. Too much tension on fan belt will cause rapid wear
e. Drive with low pressure in tires
f. Drive into a curve in high gear to cause excessive tire wear
g. "Ride" the clutch to increase wear
h. Do not refill radiator completely
i. Increase gas consumption by continuously driving in low gear

j. Wear out brake linings by constant use of brakes instead of using lower gear
k. Wear out engine by constantly driving slowly in high gear or driving at high speeds in too low a gear

How can you quickly set fire to a motor vehicle?

a. Burning newspapers under hood
b. Soak rags in gas or oil, set them on fire and throw under hood

Metal spike impedes motor vehicle traffic
Left: Metal spike (compare its size with match and match box)
Right: Emplacement of spike
Manufacture: Take a small piece of steel about 12 to 15 centimeters long and 5 to 8 millimeters in diameter. File both ends to sharp points. Cut both ends with hacksaw about 3 to 5 centimeters. The four parts (They are only held together in the middle section for about 5 centimeters) are now bent outward. Though the spike may fall to the ground in any position one point will always be up. The strength of the spike and the length of each point are sufficient to penetrate even the heaviest truck tires.
Use:
a. Spread on streets (especially at night)
b. Lay immediately in front of tires of parked vehicles (conceal spike by pushing it under tire).

10. Ambushing Individual Vehicles

Fire upon the driver and the assistant driver with an air rifle. With this type of weapon the shot can be hardly heard. However, the force of projectile is great enough to wound them so that you can dispose of them right afterward with a bayonet.

By minimizing noise you gain time and can remove material

Ambush of a single enemy vehicle

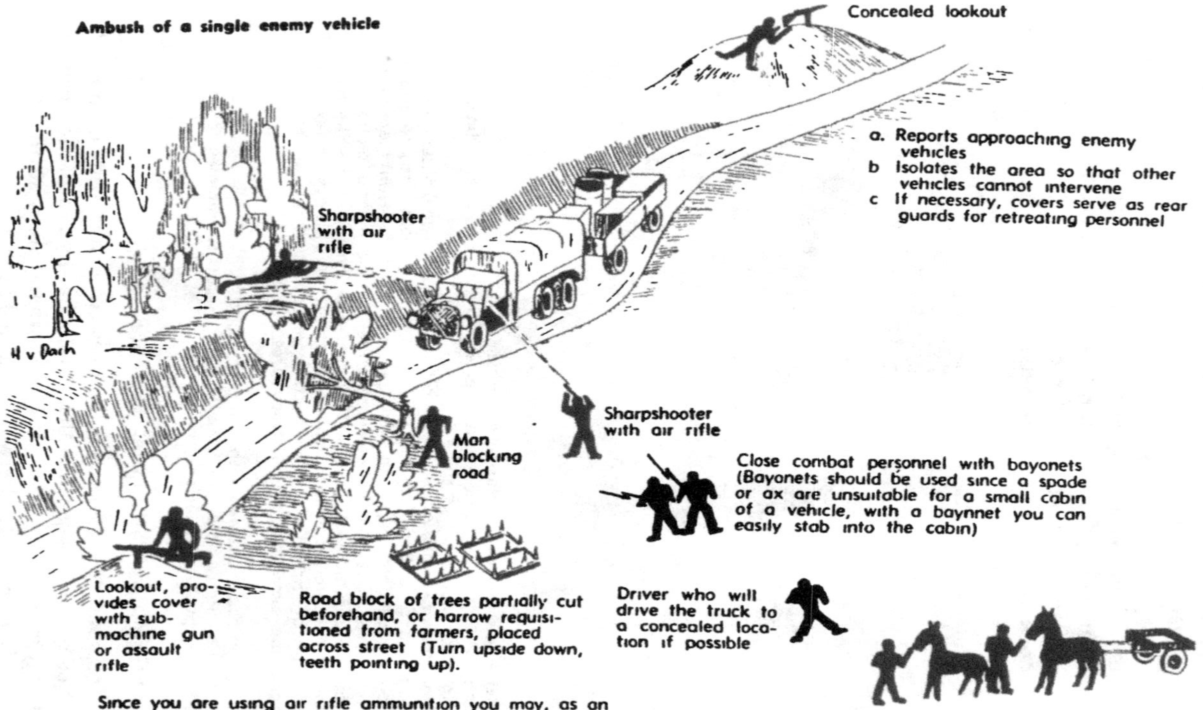

Since you are using air rifle ammunition you may, as an exception, post sharpshooters on both sides of the road. With conventional ammunition you must never do this in order not to endanger your own personnel.

from the truck less hurriedly. If deemed feasible, you have the truck driven to a concealed location (forest, etc.) by one of your drivers in order to examine the loot. Dead enemy personnel must be taken along and buried.

A collection section always immediately follows the assault element. This section removes all usable items and quickly withdraws to pre-designated rally points, often before the fight is completely finished. Thus the withdrawal of this section is covered by the continuing fire fight.

11. Raiding Enemy Columns

Normally the enemy will be paralyzed by your raid. Nevertheless, you have to take into consideration that he may react by attacking you out of despair or due to an especially forceful leader.

Consequently, you must have a safe route of withdrawal, either utilizing terrain features which make enemy pursuit difficult, or using mines.

In our mountainous terrain, raids with light machine guns, machine guns, and mortars upon transport columns on roads, marching columns and trains promise to be successful, even from a great distance.

As the commander, you must clarify the following points before the raid:

a. Time of initiating fire
   (1) Upon your orders
   (2) Opening fire by one lead weapon (then all others commence firing)
   (3) Automatically, when the head of the column has reached a certain point in the terrain
b. Stop the lead vehicle:
   (1) By felling a tree
   (2) Mines
   (3) By firing upon it
c. Distribute your fire throughout the column:
   (1) Determine who fires on the front portion of column
   (2) Determine who fires on the center of column
   (3) Determine who fires on the end of column
   (When using mortars, have them commence firing only when the entire column has stopped.)
d. Signal for discontinuing the fire fight:
   (1) Bugle calls
   (2) Flares

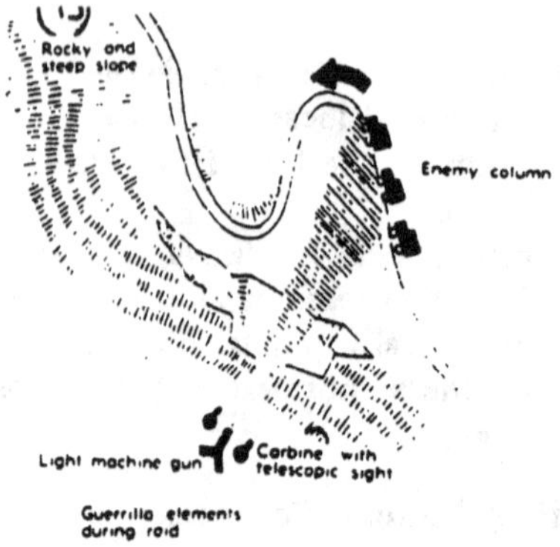

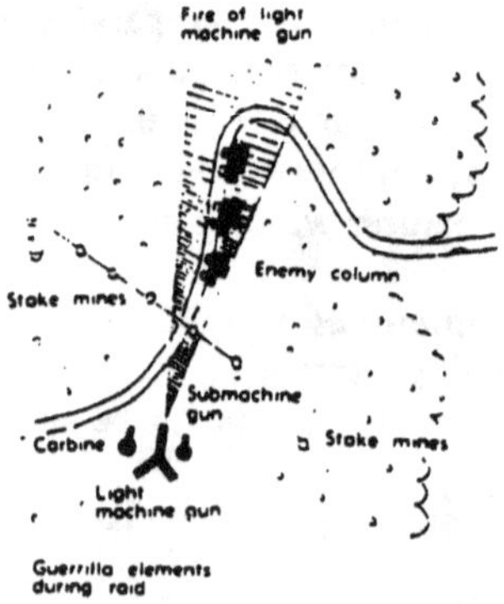

(3) Withdrawal according to time (for instance, five minutes after commencing fire)

e. After discontinuing the fight, personnel will return singly, and using separate paths, to predesignated rally point.

12. Surprise Attacks

A. General

a. Reconnaissance by commander of guerrilla detachment:
   (1) Observation through binoculars
   (2) Evaluate photos, drawings of objective
   (3) Obtain information from workers employed at installations in order to select the most critical targets, to obtain information needed to calculate demolition changes and to determine the most desirable firing positions.

b. Briefing detachment commanders in the area concerned (possibilities):
   (1) Have them observe the installation from a distance through binoculars,

(2) Brief them with photos or sketches,

(3) Stroll by close to the installation posing as a harmless "civilian going for a walk" (bicyclists or motor vehicle drivers repairing something, farm laborers mowing, digging, etc.).

c. Operational plan

(1) The plan of the detachments must be as simple as possible.

(2) They will usually operate in three parties:

(a) Raiding party (eliminates the guards or at least keeps them pinned down);

(b) Technical party (responsible for demolitions);

(c) Reserve (isolates the scene of fighting, fires upon relief elements from well prepared, concealed positions).

d. Implementation of Operation

(1) Keep the plan secret from your own people until shortly before the operation. Only confide in those

Disposing of guards without any noise.

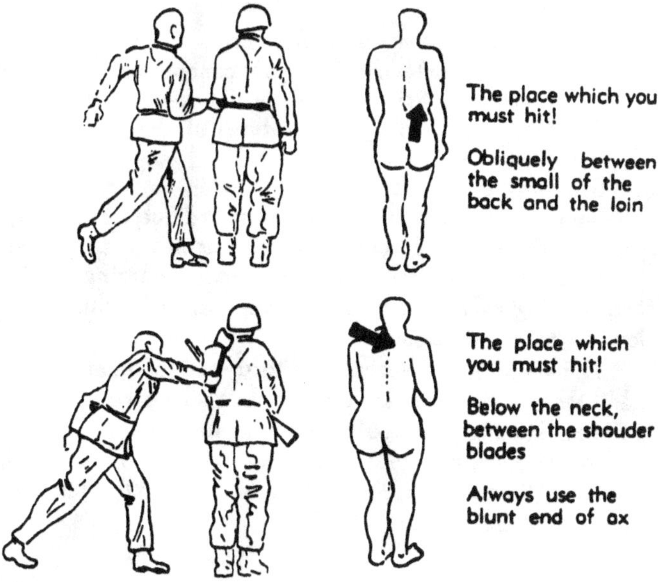

people whose assistance is indispensable for the preparations (NCO's).

(2) Approach the objective quickly during the night, avoiding roads.

(3) Occupy a well covered position near the objective where you will wait for the following night (attack). At this time, brief the entire detachment about the plan.

(4) Favorable time to commence operation: Shortly after night sets in. Thus you can brief your personnel on the terrain during dusk. The operation will be conducted under the cover of darkness. The largest portion of the night will then be available to withdraw.

B. Reconnaissance of enemy security system

a. Determine location of guard house. Report to any guard with an inaccurate pass or invent some other pretext so that you will be led to the guard house to clarify the matter. If you keep your eyes open, you will be able not only to find out the location of the guard house, but also to draw some conclusions as to numbers of guards and alertness of the enemy.

b. Determine when the guard is changed. Observe changing of the guard during the day from a distance through binoculars; at night from close up (i.e., apartment opposite the installation).

c. Determine weapon emplacements of guards. If they are so well camouflaged that you cannot make them out with binoculars, figure out where the enemy must have emplaced them by studying the features of the terrain surrounding the installation.

C. Disposing of guards

Study the habits of personnel on guard duty. Especially times of relief, guard posts and routes and pecularities in their behavior.

Unfavorable weather (biting cold, paralyzing heat, stinging heat, stinging rain) will facilitate your plans by reducing the general alertness of guard personnel.

The simplest and surest way to dispose of guards noiselessly is to kill them with an ax. Do not use the sharp edge but the blunt end of the ax. Hit the guard obliquely with all your strength between the small of the back and loins or between the shoulder blades below the neck. Even in the dark you will be able to hit the place easily and without missing.

13. Attacking a Depot

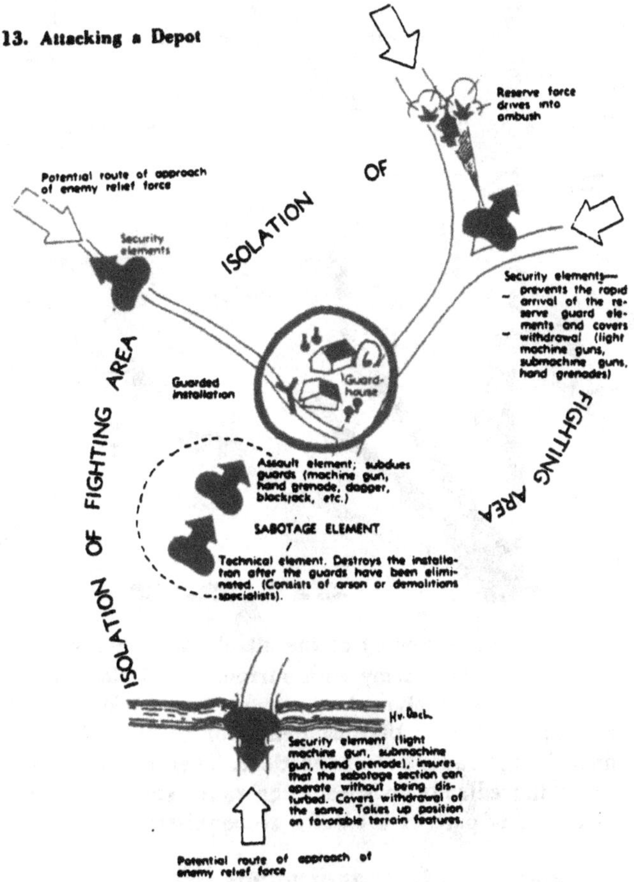

14. Surprise Attack Upon a Small Post

Divide your unit into:

a. Fighting element:
   (1) Fire support elements
   (2) Assault elements
   (3) Technical sections (i.e., wire cutting sections, obstacle demolition sections, mine clearing sections);

b. Demolition section:
   Demolition, arson

c. Loot collection section:
   (1) Light motor vehicles
   (2) Pack animals, horse drawn wagons
   (3) Civilians may be used temporarily to back pack items

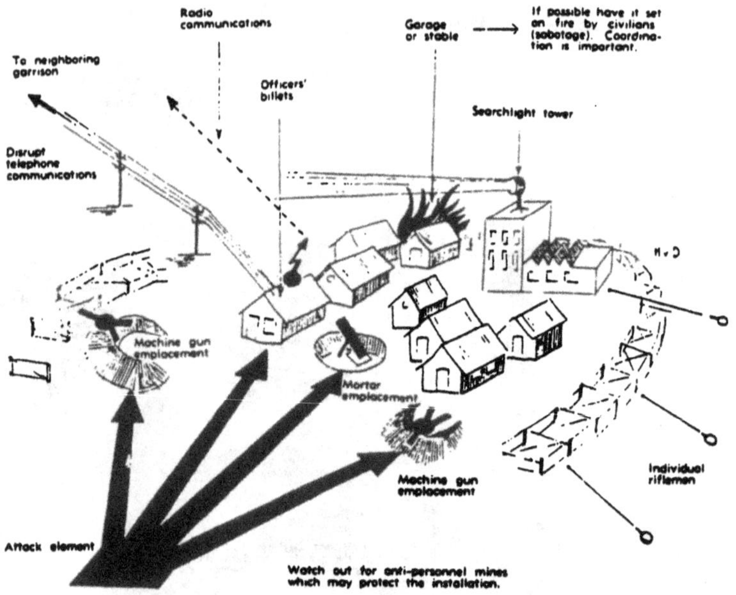

Upon commencement of the attack you must interrupt all communications of the enemy with surrounding installations (neighboring garrison) so that no help can be summoned. Cut all telephone wires leading out of the installation or cause a short circuit. You cannot disrupt radio communications. Therefore send out an assault element immediately to silence the radio station. Determination of its location is part of a careful reconnaissance.

15. Attack on a Communications Net

Possible Methods of Sabotaging Telephone Net

- Overhead Net (Overhead lines)
  - Cause short circuit
  - Pull down wires
  - Fell telephone poles by
    - cutting
    - blasting
    - knocking over
  - Complicate repairs by installing booby traps
- Underground Net (Cables)
  - Dig a hole
  - Disrupt cables at bridges
- Telephone Switchboards
  - Surprise Attack

Interruption of underground cables

Underground cables consist of several wires which are insulated against each other and against dirt (cable).

In some places, cables are inserted into iron pipes or concrete boxes to offer additional protection.

The destruction of underground cables is complicated and dangerous since you have to dig a hole and because cables normally run alongside a busy street.

In order to obtain results which are to last for some time, do the following:

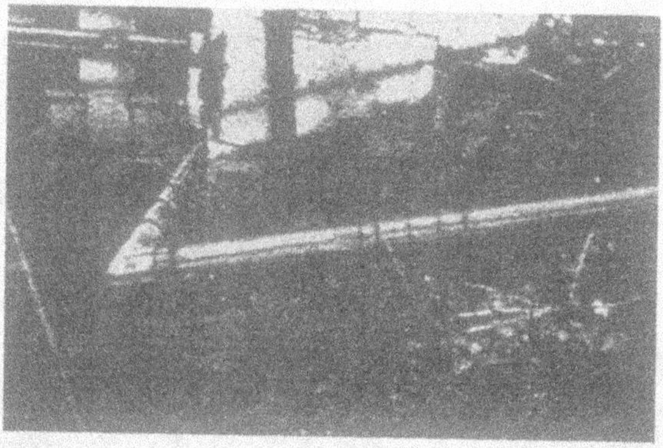

At the bridge support, the cable comes out of the ground, crosses over the water along the bridge and then reenters the ground on the opposite bank.

a. Thorough procedure—dig up the cable which is usually 80 centimeters underground. Remove the insulation and cut the cable in two. Replace the insulation, fill the hole and eliminate any traces of digging.

b. Quick procedure—dig up the cable and cut it. Prior to filling hole lay ends of cable in such a manner (if needed, weigh down with rocks) so that they do not touch each other. Cover hole and camouflage traces of digging. On the average, such an interruption will last three to four days.

Technically speaking, the best points of sabotage are where the cables cross a river. They are mostly mounted next to or underneath the bridge and can be easily cut. The disadvantage, however, is the fact that bridges are often guarded.

Interruption of overhead cables

To disrupt overhead telephone net, cut or blast poles in such a manner that wires will break. Cut or blast trees so that they will damage wires when falling. Install one or two stake mines as well as a few anti-personnel mines which will render clearing and repair more difficult.

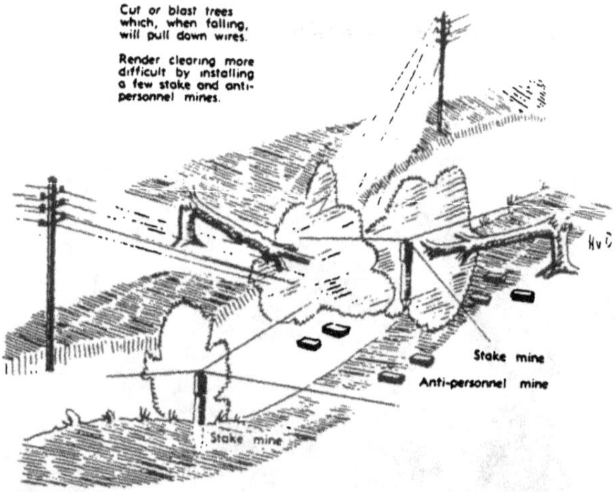

Cable

Telephone net

Be sure to destroy those cables leading to important headquarters (staff, etc). You can do this by shorting the circuits, pulling down wires, cutting wires, cutting and removing long pieces of wire.

A simple method of damaging telephone wires is to attach a short piece of metal or rock on a strong, long rope and throw it

① Cable ② Gas or water pipes

over the wires. The rope will wrap around the wires and you pull it to break them. It is best to do this in the center. between two poles, since the wire will break easiest there.

Power net

To damage high tension wires simply establish connection with the ground (ladder). if you do not have sufficient explosives to destroy the towers.

Here you need a wire. at one end of which you attach a rock or piece of iron. The other end is to be inserted into moist ground, if possible. You then throw the weighted end over the line. Caution! Release wire immediately after throwing.

Sabotage of high tension wires

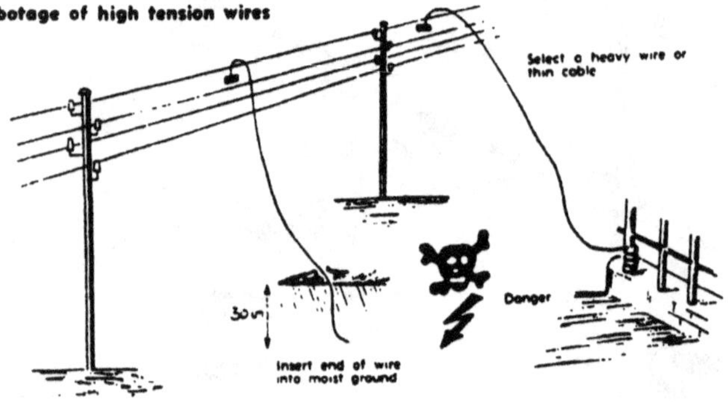

To prevent any accidents you must be able to distinguish quickly between telephone and high tension wires. Remember arrangement of insulators which never changes from the following sketch and photos.

How to distinguish between telephone and high tension wires.

To prevent losses you must be able to distinguish between the two.

Telephone wire
Insulators are parrallel

High tension wire
Insulators are staggered

16. Attacking a Railroad Net

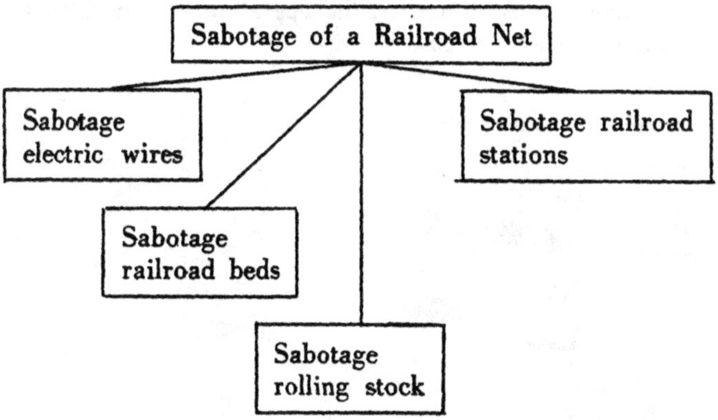

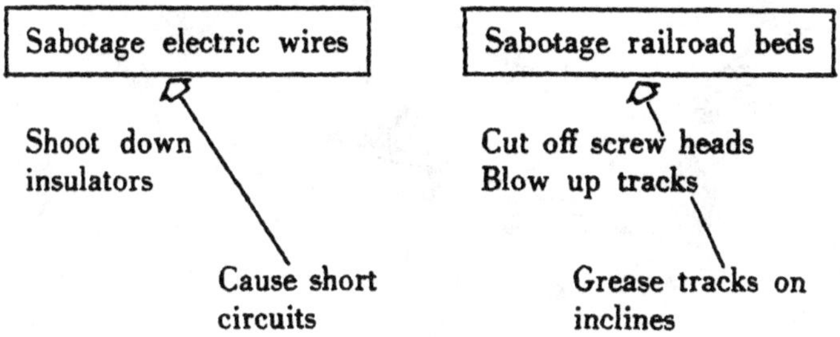

Damage electric wires

a. From an overpass:

Connect the protective railing with a track by means of a strong cable (thin wire cable)

Attach a cable (wire cable 5-8 mm) at the protective railing.

At the other end attach a piece of iron about 20 centimeters long to act as a weight.

Throw the cable onto the electric wire from the railing. Let go of cable when it is thrown, to prevent electrocuting yourself.

Since the railing and the walls of the overpass are grounded, the operation is relatively safe.

Use only strong cables. Thin cables will melt at once causing only a slight voltage reduction.

b. On an open stretch:

Attach the cable, again weighted down by a piece of iron, to the track.

Throw the cable over the wire. It is immaterial if the cable catches on the supporting wire or the electric wire proper. Both carry voltage. Immediately release the cable when throwing.

Wires are installed high. Where you are unable to throw from a steep embankment or from a roof, the operation will be difficult. If at all possible, use an overpass.

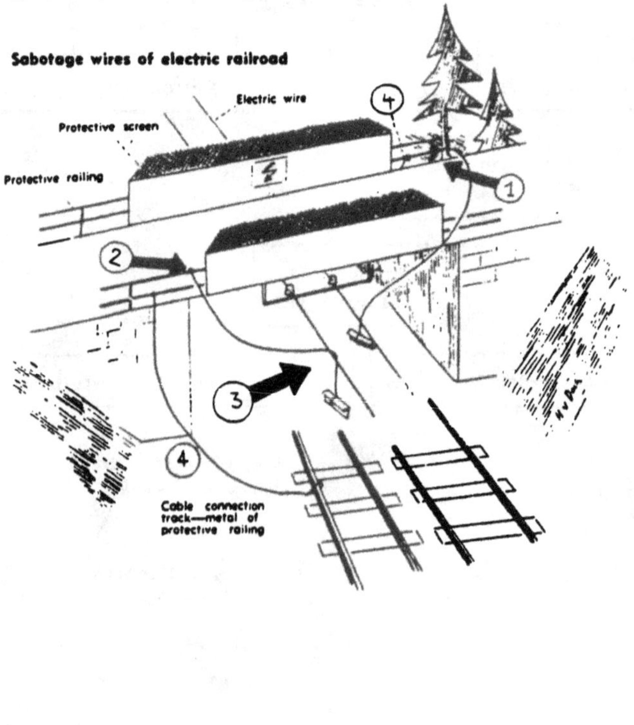

c. Shoot the insulators down with a carbine:

If possible, do this on an open stretch and far away from stations.

When using this method, you must support the weapon (i.e., a wall, the shoulder of a man) in order to hit the target quickly and without wasting a lot of valuable ammunition.

You have to distinguish between "support wire" and "electric wire." The purpose is to shoot down the "support wire" by destroying the supporting insulators and thus cause it to fall on the "support structure" (tower); you will cause a short circuit and the support wire will melt.

Maintain a safe distance (30 to 50 meters) so as not to endanger yourself by the arc caused by the falling support wire.

On dual tracks you must destroy both wires.

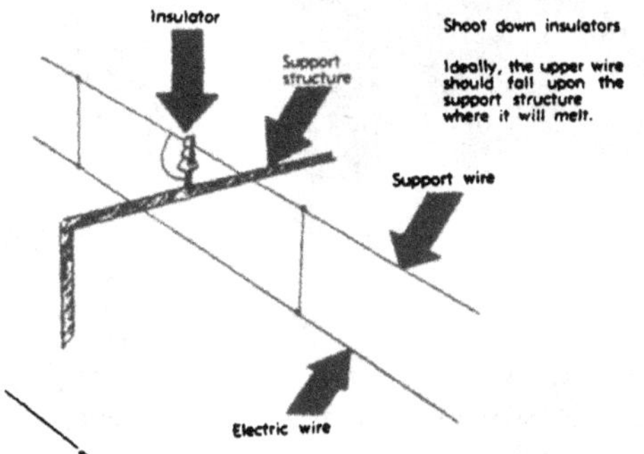

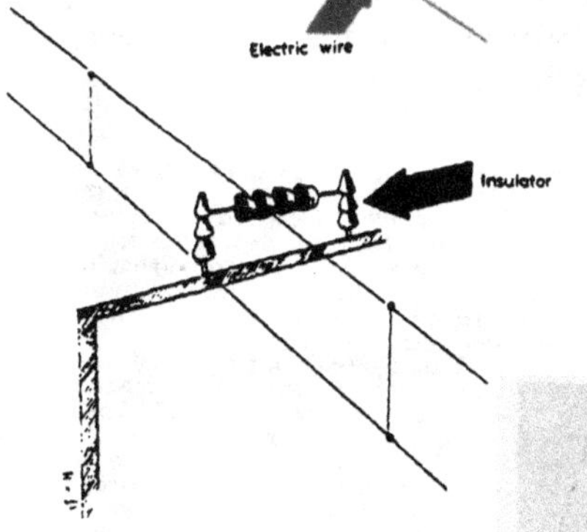

Sabotage of railroad bed (track system)

Knock off screw heads.

Screw heads can be knocked off relatively easily by using a sledge hammer. Heads will come off very easily especially when it is very cold.

Result: Do not have great expectations. This will not derail trains. However, this will consume a great deal of the enemy engineers' time and effort.

Sabotage! Knock off screw heads with sledge hammer.

Blasting of tracks

On an open stretch always destroy tracks at a curve. Always blast the outer rail. How big must the piece be that has to be blasted out of the track to cause the train to be derailed?

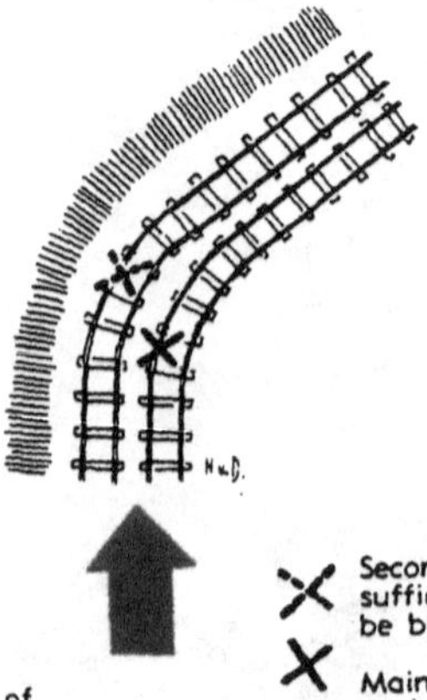

Destroy tracks on open stretch.
On an open stretch you must always blast tracks at a curve for the following two reasons:
Bent tracks are more difficult to replace by the enemy than straight ones of which he has an ample supply.
Trains derail more easily in curves than on straight stretches. Always blast the outer rail. The centrifugal force of an approaching train will derail it more easily at the blasting point and, at the same time, will throw the debris onto the neighboring tracks.

Secondary blast. Only blast when you have sufficient explosives. The outer tracks will be blocked anyhow by the detrailed train.

Main blast. If you have limited amounts of explosives, only blast the inner tracks.

Travel direction of trains: normally the train will travel on the left.

If the engineer does not notice the gap and enters the curve with full speed, it is sufficient to blast a piece of a length of 30 centimeters.

If railroad personnel are aware of the damaged track they can proceed across gaps of even 50 to 60 centimeters if they go slowly.

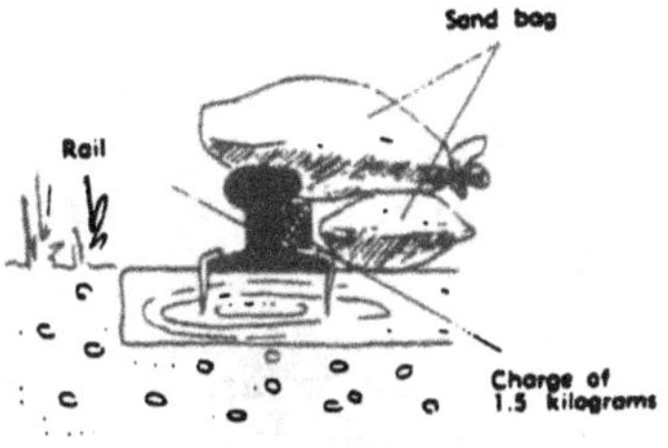

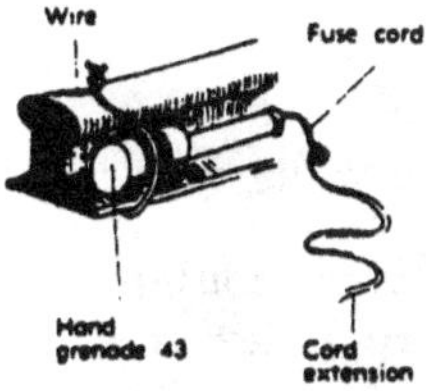

Sabotage of tracks by "greasing"

Grease tracks on inclines with grease, oil, soft soap, etc.; you thus will block the stretch.

Always grease both rails for a distance of at least 150 meters; otherwise the wheels of the engine will skid over the place by means of its own momentum or the engineer may sand the short stretch of greased track.

- **Sabotage of rolling stock**
  - **Train traps**
    - with explosive,
    - without explosive,
    - by loosening rails
  - **Individual damage**
    - blasting
    - damage axles
- **Sabotage of railroad stations**
  - **Raid**
  - **Individual damage**
    - blast switch
    - jam switch
    - damage switch house

Train traps with explosive

In order to derail transport trains you have to build "train traps" using hidden charges which are detonated the moment the engine passes the point where the charges are placed.

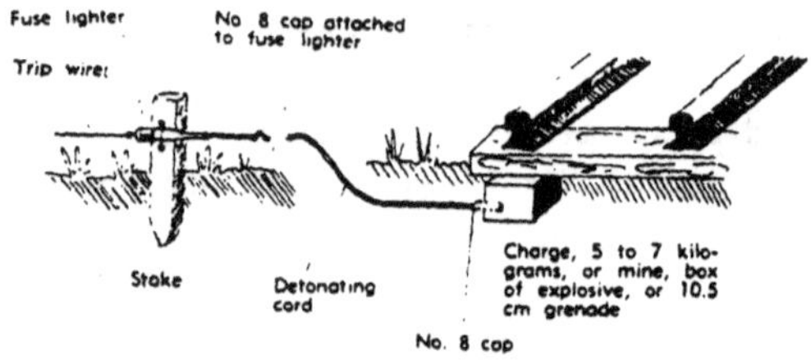

Creation of train traps by loosening rails

a. Loosen tie mountings (key, screw, nails) on eight successive ties.

b. Remove fish-plate.

c. Apply leverage and move one rail toward the inside (crow bar, etc.) and jam the fish-plate in between. Result: The train will derail.

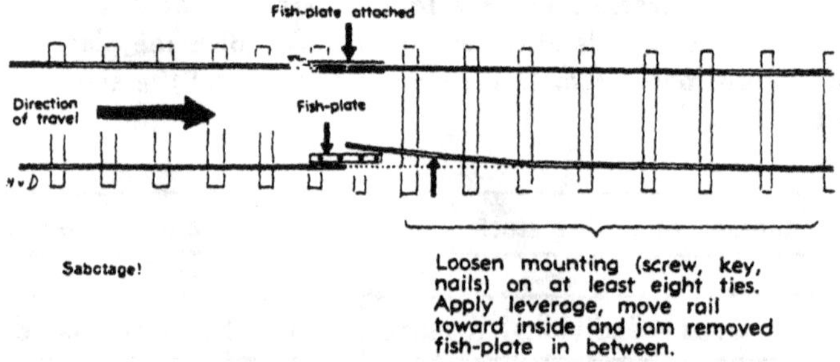

Loosen bolts of fish-plate at rail joint (four to six bolts). Remove fish-plate.

Apply leverage and move one rail to the inside; jam fish-plate in between.

Loosen tie mountings (key, screw, nails) on at least 8 successive ties.

Destruction of Rolling Stock

Most effective means (to be used when you have sufficient time) takes about three minutes per wagon axle.

Attach a charge of 1 kilogram tightly on the axle by means of two wires.

Basic rule: Careful installation of charge requires a relatively long time; however, you will obtain greater results with least amount of explosive.

When you are pressed for time, attach two demolition charges of 600 grams to a rope and hang it over the axle. To improvise, you may use two old cans of plastic or, if necessary, commercial type explosive. This requires approximately one half minute per axle.

Keep the ropes as short as possible so that charges touch the axle.

Basic rule: Hasty method with relative careless installation of charges takes little time but requires relative large amounts of explosive which produce poor results.

Destruction of Electric Engines

a. Shoot off roof insulators with carbine.
b. Destroy instrument panel in engineer cabin with a sledge hammer.
c. Destroy transformer oil containers in engine room (knock holes into the thin metal wall with a pick and set fire to oil that flows out).

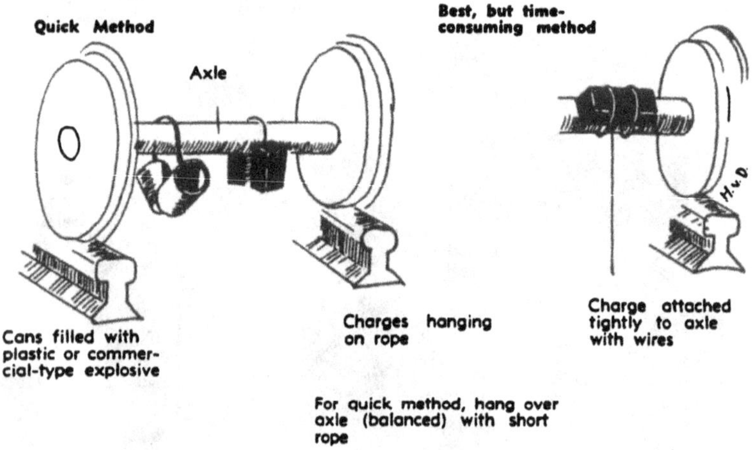

Destruction of Steam Engines

a. Throw a charge of one to two kilograms into fire-box (opening through which coal is thrown).
b. Destroy steering mechanism with sledge hammer.
c. Fire into boiler with light machine gun or machine gun (steel-core bullets).
Target: Center third of engine, about 1.5 meters in front of cabin.

Sabotage of Railroad Rolling Stock

a. Throw a handful of sand, abrassive powder, or metal shavings into each grease box.
b. Covers on grease boxes can be easily opened, especially on freight cars.
c. No immediate results will be seen. However, the bearings will soon wear out.

Since no technical know-how is required and because of the simplicity of the operation, everybody can do it, i.e., railroad employee when checking cars, or laborers loading or unloading cars.

Throw a handful of sand, abrasive powder, or metal shavings into each grease box.

Raiding a Railroad Station

A railroad station consists of the following targets:

a. Station building; bottom floor with office and small switch house, first floor with living quarters of station master (at larger stations the switch house is installed in a separate building next to or above the tracks).

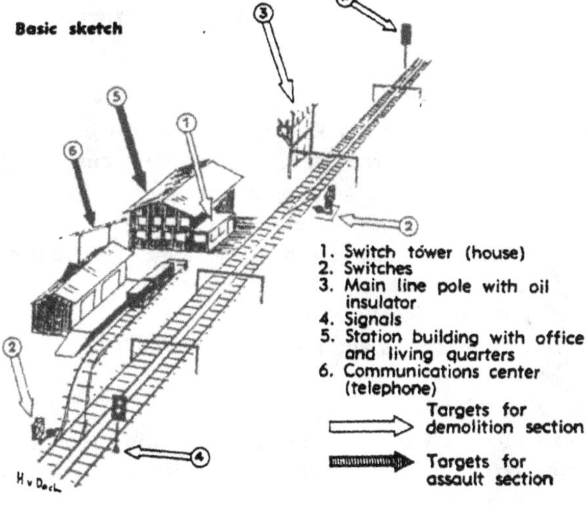

b. Tracks: Rails, switches, frogs, cross ties, and perhaps turn tables.
c. Overhead wire: Main line pole with oil insulator.
d. Signals: Signals at entrance and exit.
e. Communications center (official and commercial): Civilian telephone, railroad telephone, telegraph in office, i.e., main building.

How to divide the guerrilla detachment:

a. Raiding party—interrupts the telephone and telegraph communication, keeps railroad personel under control, and eliminates any guards.
b. Demolition party—destroys technical installations.
c. Reserve—isolates the objective, ambushes any enemy reserve force which might arrive and covers withdrawal of raiding and demolition parties.

Demolition: Place a 1 kilogram charge at spot indicated by arrow.

Order of Priority in Destruction

a. If you have limited time:
   (1) Blast switches with 1 kilogram of explosive.
   (2) Blast switch tower with concentrated charge (hand grenade 43 with additional charge).
b. If you have more time:
   (1) Also blast the main line pole as well as frog and center pieces of tracks.
   (2) If you have plenty of time:
   Also blast signals and cut wires to switches, signals and gates.
c. Destruction of switches:
   Sabotage: Jam a wooden or metal wedge into the place indicated by arrow. The switch cannot be fully operated and the

train will derail. (Be careful! This method can only be used with the approval of the station personnel since personnel operating the switches would soon find out said switches were not functioning properly.)

Destruction of switches

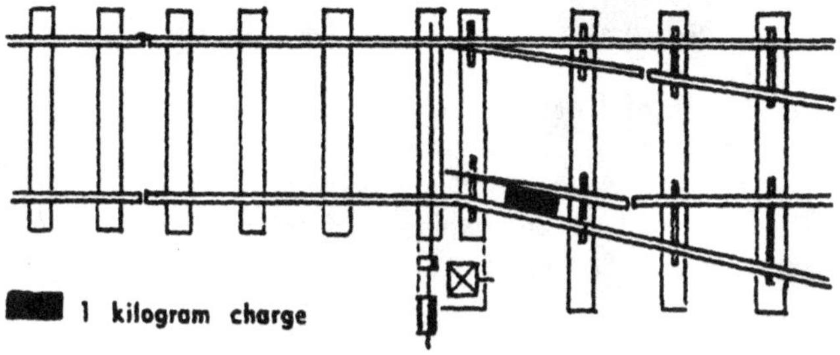

d. Destruction of main Line Pole:
The pole is usually located across from the station building. If pressed for time fire into the oil insulator with a carbine. If you have more time, blast the pole at location indicated by arrow.

Destruction of main pole (usually across from station building)
If you have little time: fire into the oil insulator (1).
If you have sufficient time: blast the pole at place (2) indicated by arrow.

e. Destruction of frogs:
   Place a charge of 1 kilogram at location by arrow.
f. Damage switches without explosive:
   If you do not have any explosive, destroy the switch mechanism with a sledge hammer.

Sabotage switches! If you do not have any explosive, destroy the switch mechanism with a sledge hammer or bend it with a crow bar.

Interdicting Railroad Lines

Procedure

a. Ascertain the most favorable points to be attacked.

b. Find a concealed approach to railway for sabotage personnel.

A simple break in the track will, on the average, result in interruption of traffic: five to six hours for main lines (normally repaired at once by the enemy); six to eight hours for secondary lines (longer interruption since not repaired at once by enemy); twelve to thirteen hours by train derailments on main and secondary lines.

Security of railways only becomes effective when a guard is posted every one hundred meters.

As a counter measure against railroad sabotage, the enemy will reduce speed limits for trains. Consequently, normally only the engine and the first three or four cars will be derailed; this reduces damage to the railway bed and to the rolling stock.

But don't be too depressed. By virtue of the reduced speed limit you will still obtain the following results, even though results are not immediately visible: longer use of lines by increased travel time of trains; a reduction in line efficiency when adding up these individual delays.

This "safety measure" causes the enemy other problems.

Increase in travel time is especially a nuisance to the enemy either during offensive operations or during critical phases of defensive operations.

Therefore it is important for guerrilla units to maintain communications with their own army or allies, even though located hundreds or even thousands of kilometers from the front, in order to coordinate guerrilla with conventional operations. Monitoring radio frequencies may provide guide lines for planning such operations.

Large scale offensives will allow each guerrilla unit to commence or increase offensive operations since the enemy can now be harrassed more safely than ever before, as he has less means of defending himself against you.

Interruption of railroad line*

(Example: Interrupting traffic between Bern and Thun)

Right

Detour via secondary routes impossible

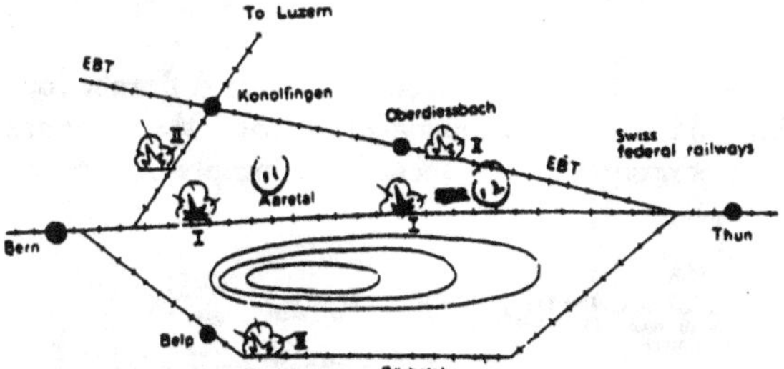

I Primary demolitions on main line

II Secondary demolitions are emplaced to prevent rerouting of critical material. Secondary demolitions are detonated at the same time or about one half hour after the main line is cut.

*Luzern, Konolfingen, Oberdiessbach, Bern, Thun, Belp, are Swiss towns. Aaretal and Guerbetal are names of Swiss valleys.

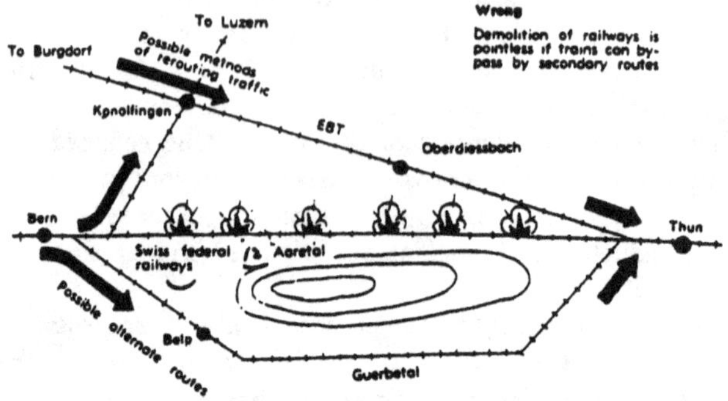

It is important to create confusion in the rail system by causing abnormal train schedules; to delay traffic for increasingly long periods of time.

You can do this by keeping the maintenance organization continually busy; (alerting repair teams, making up repair trains, etc.); having something happen every day. Over the long run, it is more demoralizing and nerve wracking for the enemy to make smaller repairs without interruption than infrequent major ones.

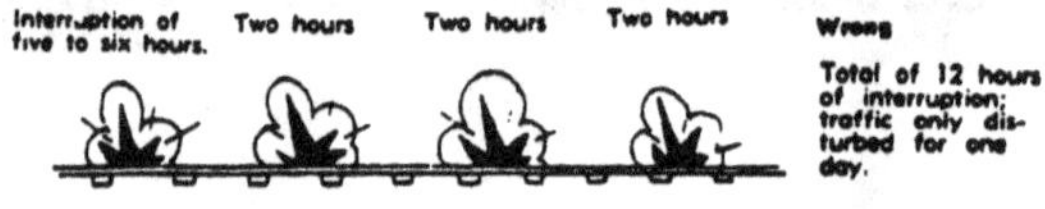

It is wrong to interdict tracks on four different locations on the same day and during the same operation. Maintenance crews then have to be committed only once. They simply repair one point after another.

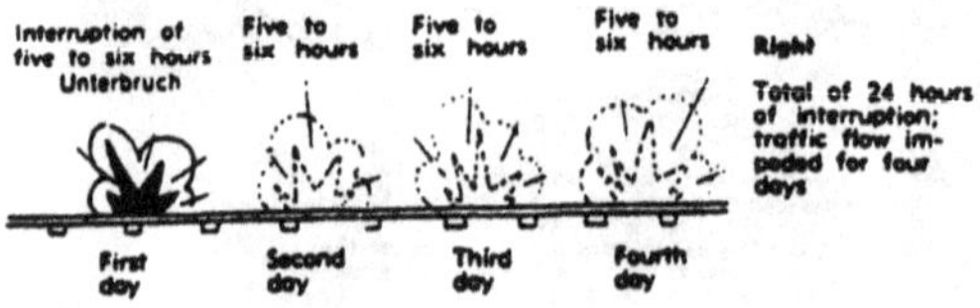

It is much more effective to interrupt one length of track on four consecutive days. The entire maintenance organization has to start anew each time. The traffic flow is impeded on four days. Confusion is thus greater, and the total period of interruption is almost twice as long.

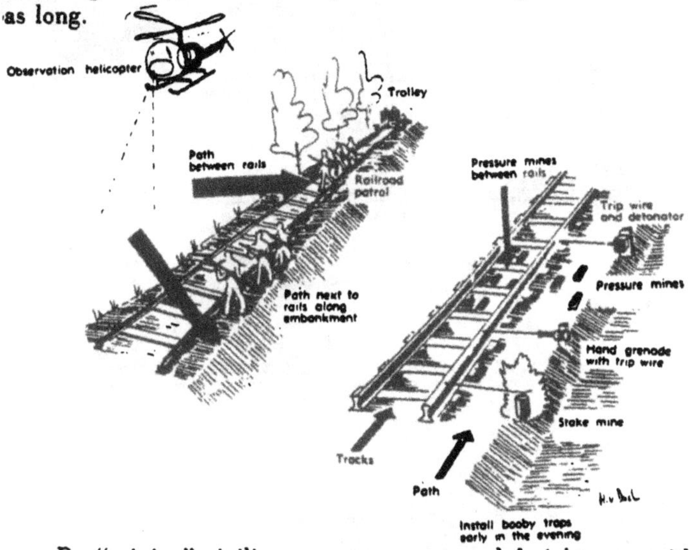

By "mixing" civilian passenger cars and freight cars with war material or troops, the enemy attempts to keep you from sabotaging railways. The civilians on the train serve as protective cover for the enemy.

By pushing empty freight cars or cars with sand in front of the train ("protected" trains), the enemy will attempt to protect his valuable engines against train traps.

In addition, by mounting anti-aircraft guns on trains ("protected" and "armed" trains), the enemy is able to defend himself against guerrilla raiding parties.

Fighting Railroad Patrols

Guarding a railroad can be done by the enemy as follows: flying helicopters at low altitude; use of trolleys; patrolling along railways.

Stopping Deportation Trains

(Same procedure applied with motor vehicle transports.) Do not derail the train as you do not wish to injure persons being deported. Consequently, you have to block the railway but in such a manner as to prevent enemy foot patrols, personnel on trolleys or in helicopters from detecting anything unusual.

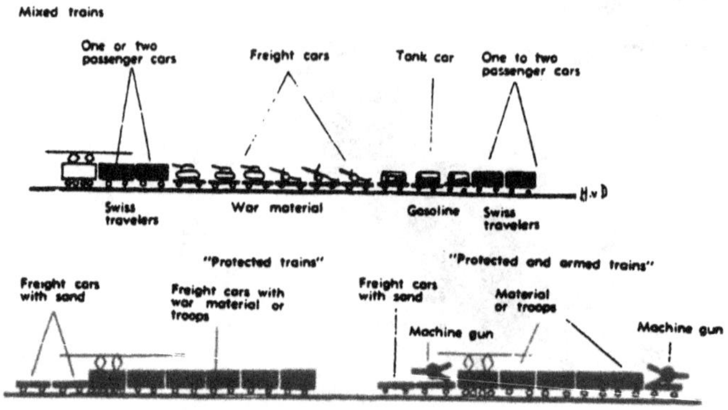

The block becomes effective just prior to the arrival of an approaching train.

The block will be noticed early enough by train personnel to stop the train in time and to prevent derailment or hitting the block.

On the other hand, the train personnel does not have enough time to stop at a great distance and back out of the ambush area.

It is best to use big trees which are blasted across the tracks and the overhead wire when the train approaches.

If you do not have any explosive, drive one or two heavily loaded trucks across the tracks filled with sand, dirt, or rocks.

Assign raiding parties to eliminate train guards.

Organize the escape of the deportees before the operation. Determine how you will transport and treat the sick and injured; how you will handle injured personnel that cannot be moved.

Determine routes of withdrawal; methods of securing withdrawal.

For the operation proper you will organize your guerrilla detachment as follows: interdiction element will block the tracks with explosive, or loaded trucks; raiding party will eliminate train guards with light machine gun, machine gun, submachine gun, hand grenade; special element will instruct the liberated deportees in proper behavior. They will administer first aid to enable injured to be transported, improvise stretchers, supply food.

Loot collection party collects weapons, ammunition, clothing and equipment from dead train guards, also perhaps one to two pack animals or a small motor vehicle.

Those able and willing to fight will be incorporated into your guerrilla detachment. They will be armed and equipped with enemy material.

Those unable to fight are hidden from the enemy by placing them with reliable inhabitants.

The above mentioned method can only be used during mass deportations. The first transports will slip by. Unfortunately, a certain "initial phase" for this type of operation is indispensable. By systematic observation, however, you will be able to determine the enemy's methods of transport and those routes on which deportations will take place. You may then initiate rescue operations.

Train traps

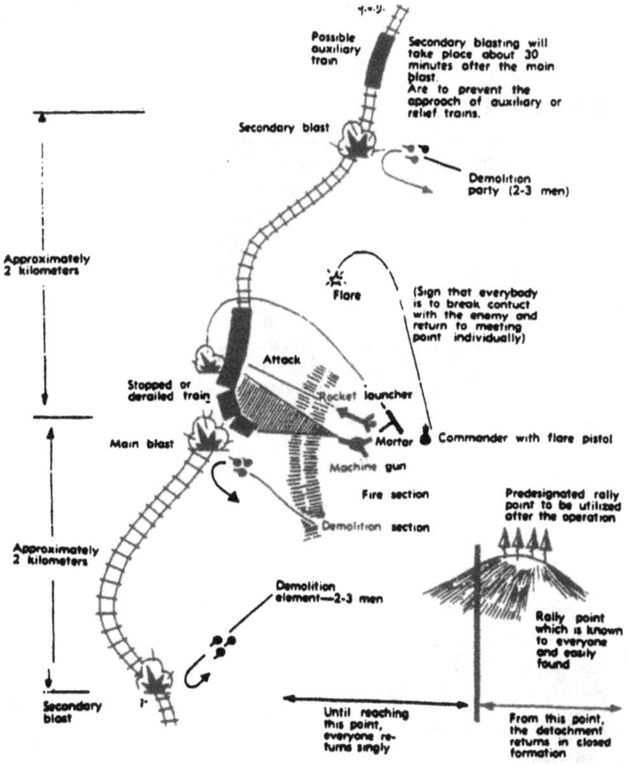

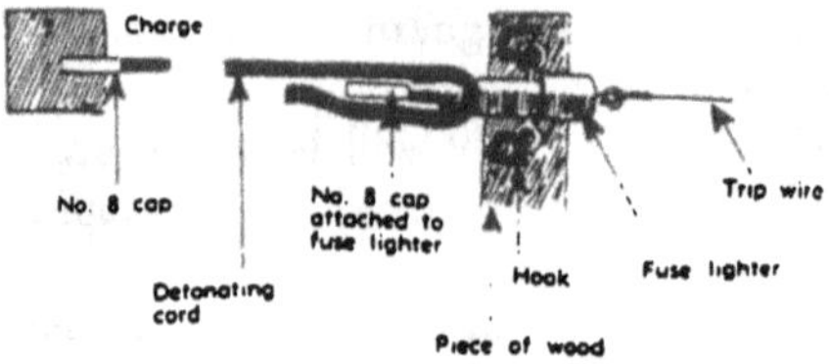

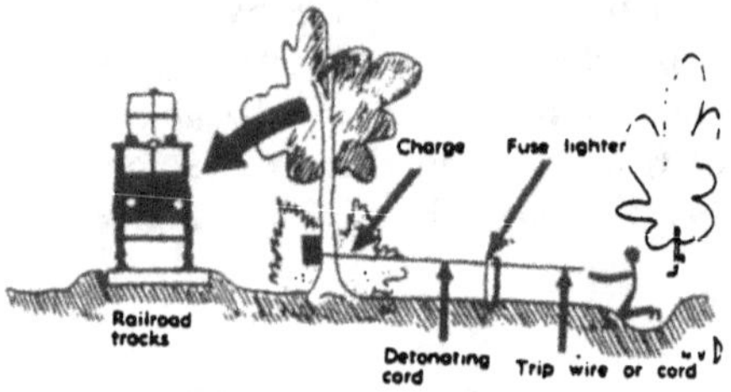

17. Attacking the Power Net

Sabotage of Power Net

- **Direct Method**
  - Wire Net
    - The large cross-country high-tension wires → Blast poles
    - Local high-tension wires → Shoot down insulators; Cause short-circuit; Fell poles by cutting, pulling down or blasting
  - Transformer Stations → Raid
- **Indirect Method**
  - Power Stations
    - Sabotage of turbines
    - Sabotage of pressure lines → i.e. blasting
    - Sabotage of dams is practically impossible

Raid on Transformer Station

A transformer station consists of the following:

a. Attendant's house:

On the bottom floor a large room with control and switch equipment; on the first floor the attendants' living quarters for employees that have to attend constantly to the equipment.

b. Fence:

To prevent accidents, normally a two to two and one half meter high wire meshing and barbed wire surrounds the entire installation.

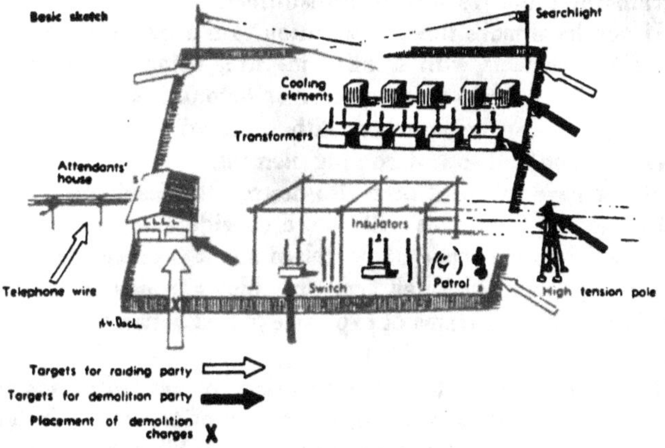

c. Searchlights:

A system of searchlights is installed on poles within the installation which illuminates the entire installation so that work can be performed even at night.

d. High tension poles:

Power supply by means of high tension poles. The last pole usually is located in the immediate vicinity of the fence (closer than 100 meters).

e. Transformers and accessories:

Includes transformers, cooling elements, switches and insulators; all of which are located in the open. Telephone to the attendant's house.

Assignment of guerrilla detachment

1. Assault element breaches fence of installation by demolition charge or wire cutters; interrupts telephone communications to attendant's house (also guard house); shoots out all searchlights in operation; eliminates guards; guards employees of the transformer station.

2. Demolition element destroys the technical installations.

3. Security element isolates the installation by preventing reinforcements from arriving; covers the withdrawal of the raiding and demolition parties.

If time is limited, destroy the transformers. They are the "nerve center" of the entire installation. Since there are relatively few transformers, this job will not take long. Transformers are protected by a metal wall about 10 millimeters thick.

Destroy them with small arms fire, using armor piercing ammunition, anti-tank rifles or rocket launchers; or detonate about 4 kilograms of explosive on the transformer.

If you have more time, in addition to the transformers, destroy the cooling elements with small arms fire, using ball ammunition, anti-tank rifles, or rocket launchers; or detonate 2 kilograms of explosives which can be attached with rope, wire, or hooks halfway between bottom and top of cooling element.

If you have sufficient time also destroy the insulators. Since you will find lots of these, this will take a considerable amount of time. These insulators are made of porcelain about 3 centimeters thick.

Destroy them with small arms fire, blows from a sledge hammer or by detonating 200 grams of explosive placed between each insulator disc.

If you have unlimited time also destroy the switch installation and high tension wires carrying the power of the entire installation by detonating three individual charges of 1 kilogram of explosive for each switch.

Overall view of a transformer station

Detailed sketch of charges and fuses used

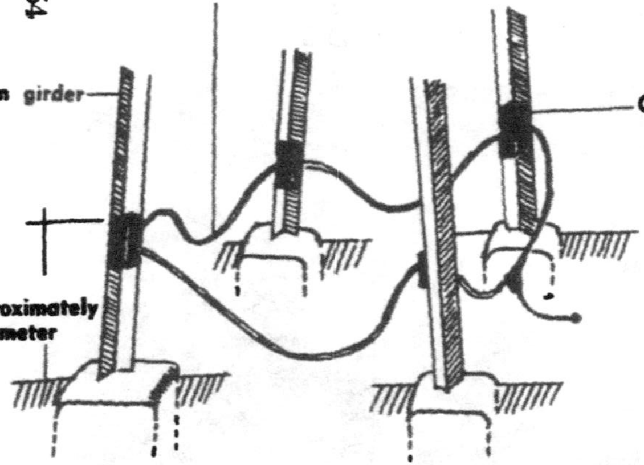

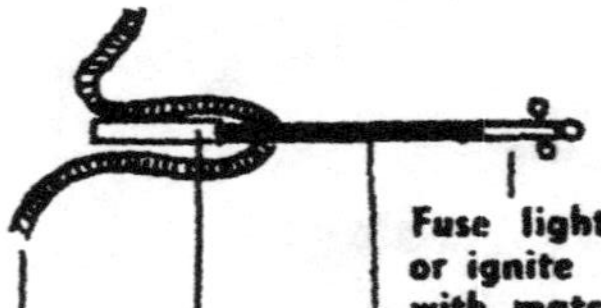

Details on emplacing detonating system

Method of emplacing charge

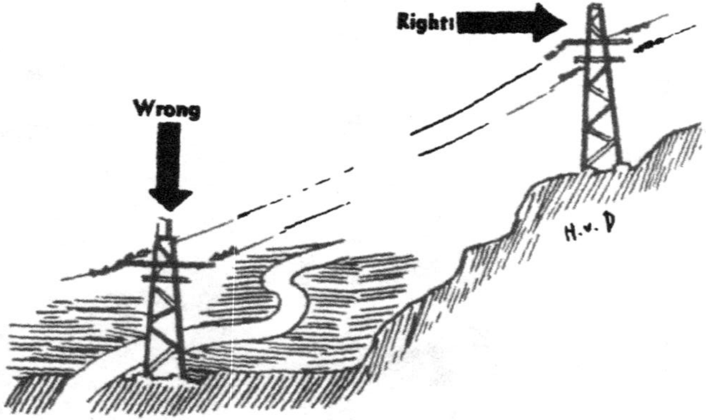

Demolition of cross-country high tension poles

Wrong: Do not blast a pole in flat country and next to a road as enemy is able to repair damages relatively easy.
Right: Blast in a remote area and in difficult terrain (steep slope) so that the enemy will have great difficulties in transporting material and traveling to the site.
Whenever possible, blast where the distance between individual poles is very great, such as rivers, ravines, etc.

18. Suprise Attack on a Fuel Depot

This applies to installations above ground. As a rule, fuel depots are located in the vicinity of railroad stations and are connected to them by means of rail sidings.

On the ground floor of the attendants' house a refueling point for tank trucks is located behind a ramp.

The 2nd floor contains attendants' quarters. The depot has surface tanks (capacity of up to several million litters—these are part of the installation) and underground tanks (accessible by a manhole) as well as a refueling installation (at the railroad track to empty rail tank cars).

There is a telephone to attendants' quarters as well as the guard house. The fence around installation is of simple construction and by no means as strong as that protecting a transformer station.

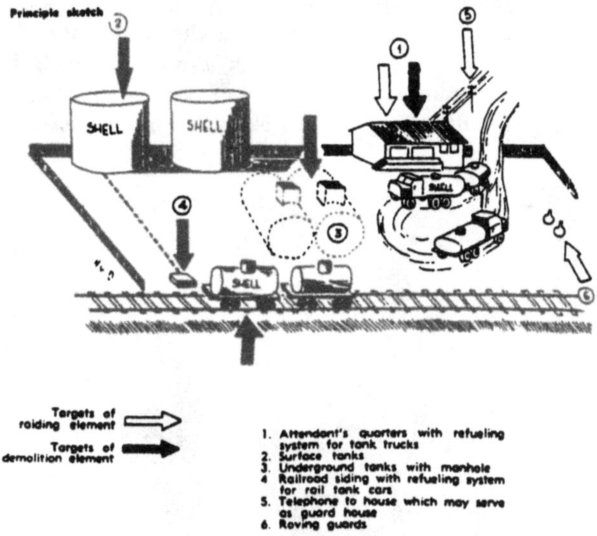

Responsibilities of Guerrilla Detachment:

1. Assault element cuts phone lines, eliminates guards and guard station attendant.
2. Demolition element will destroy technical installations including any rail tank cars on the siding.
3. Security element will isolate the installation, ambush rein-

forcements, and cover the withdrawal of the raiding and demolition elements.

Priorities of Destruction

If pressed for time, only destroy the surface and underground tank installations.

If you have sufficient time, also destroy the refueling system for tank trucks and rail cars.

Destroy tank installations and tank cars in the open with anti-tank rifle or rocket launcher, or detonate at least 4 kilograms of explosive at the bottom of the tanks.

If the tank does not explode, it will be necessary to set fire to the fuel.

This may be done by using tracer ammunition, flares, hand grenades or using anti-tank guns or rocket launchers.

Normally tanks are buried one to three meters underground. Detonate a charge in the manhole, directly on the tank wall. If the tanks are full the explosion will rupture the tank walls since the liquid cannot be compressed. If the tank is not completely full, the empty space often contains fuel vapor-air mixture which may explode. In any case the charge has to be placed on the outside of the tank.

Manhole to underground fuel tank

Open the 5 millimeter thick cover with key taken from the captured depot attendant. Destroy by detonating 400 gram charge placed upon the key hole.

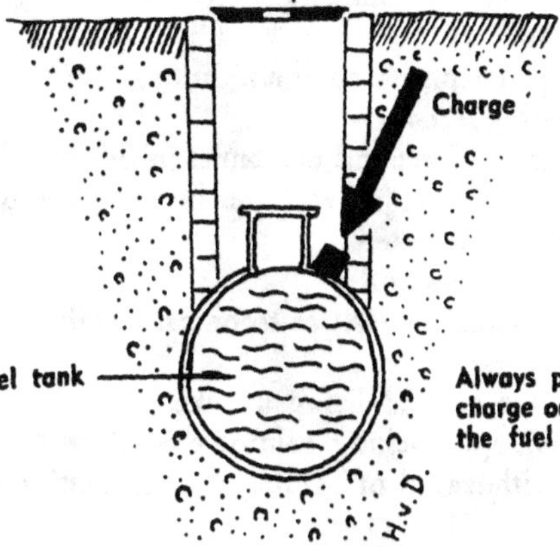

Refueling point used to empty rail tank cars

Rail tank car

Destroy with anti-tank rifle or rocket launcher. If necessary use 500 gram charge at place indicated by arrow. If the tank car does not explode at least the fuel will leak out.
Opening is similar to that used for underground tank
To destroy, detonate one kilogram charge next to refueling system.

19. Raid Against an Airfield

Assignment of Guerrilla Detachment

a. Assault element will:
   (1) Interrupt telephone communications;
   (2) Eliminate guards;
   (3) Kill flight and ground personnel in billets;
   (4) Destroy AA and searchlight installations of the airfield defensive system.

b. Demolition elements will:
   (1) Destroy planes as well as technical installations.

c. Security elements will:
   (1) Isolate the airfield being attacked;
   (2) Fight off approaching reinforcements;
   (3) Cover withdrawal of raiding and demolition elements.

Priorities of Destruction

If pressed for time, only destroy planes on the ground.

If you have sufficient time, also destroy radar and radio installations.

If you have unlimited time, also destroy fuel depots and repair shops.

Methods of Destroying Equipment and Material on an Airfield

a. Airplanes—detonate a charge of 1 kilogram on the fuselage directly behind the cockpit.

b. Radar installations—detonate a charge of 3 kilograms on the rotation mechanism of the antenna; a 2 kilogram charge on the instrument panel.

c. Repair shops—detonate charge of at least 5 kilograms in the center of the repair shop, or set fire by using gasoline, petroleum, oil and grease which you will probably find in the shop.

d. Fuel depots—see "Destruction of fuel depots."

e. AA guns—throw a hand grenade 43 into gun barrel.

f. Searchlights—fire into mirror; place a 1 kilogram charge at turning mechanism; destroy generator with concentrated charge of 2 to 3 kilograms.

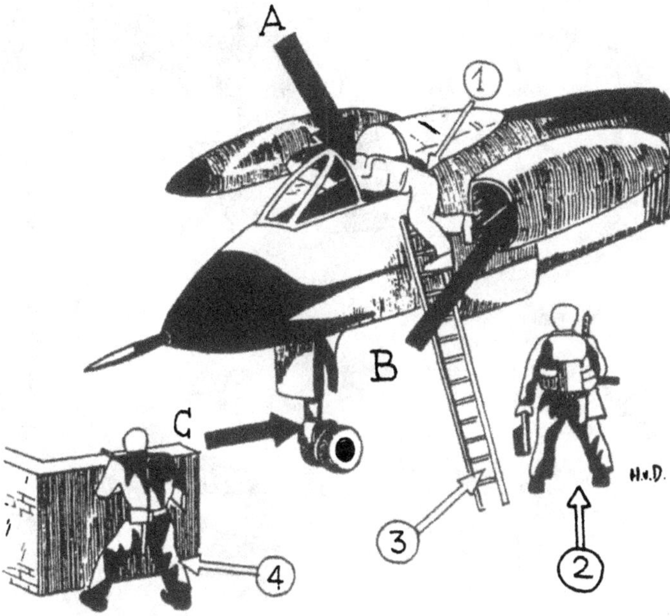

Destruction of a jet

1. Demolition expert carries carbine, ladder, wire, and places charge in plane.
2. Bearer with submachine gun carries a certain number of loosely packed, prepared charges in rucksack.
3. Ladder, approximately 3 meters long. Without this, you will be unable to reach the greatest points of vulnerability.
4. Team leader carries machine gun, hand grenade, and eliminates, if necessary, any guards. Covers his two team members during placement of charges.

Possible means of destruction. Favorable points.

A. Place incendiary canisters in pilot's seat. Unless acquainted with particular aircraft, you will have to force open the roof of the cockpit with an ax or crowbar. Noise is inevitable.

B. Air intake of jet engine. Throw a hand grenade 43 or a demolition charge into the intake which will cause heavy damage to wings, engine, or fuselage.

C. Landing gear or landing gear housing on top. Place demolition charge of 500 grams at nose wheel, as well as at wheels under wings.

Principle sketch

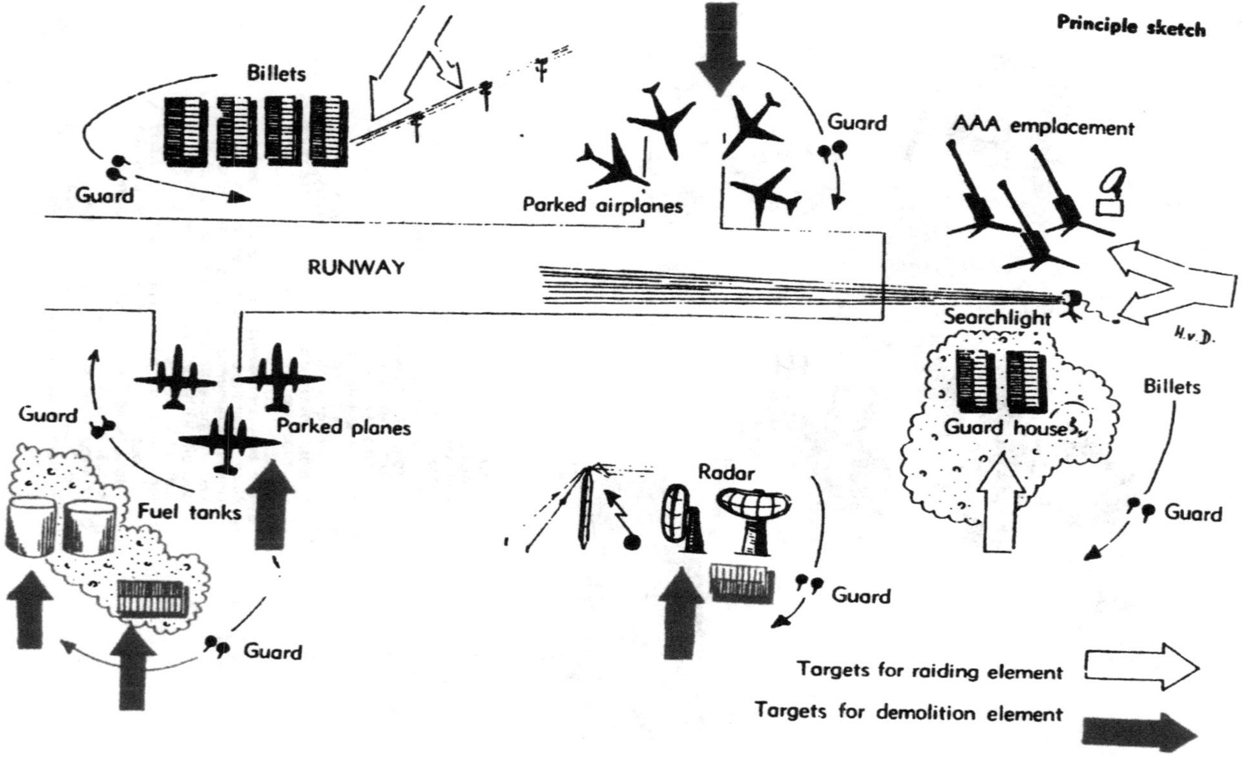

20. Destroying a Bridge

Important bridges will be demolished by our retreating troops. Guerrilla detachments will be in position to destroy "auxiliary bridges" built by the enemy. These will normally be of wooden or metal construction.

Wooden bridges:

Place hasty charges—pole charges, bangalore torpedo—across the roadway. If there are extension beams, use normal explosives.

If you have sufficient time, also destroy the abutments.

Metal bridges:

If pressed for time, use hasty charges; only destroy the beams.

If you have sufficient time, destroy according to plan; cut the bridge by simply cross sectioning it.

Blasting:

Both of the lower beams; one upper beam; one diagonal strut on the same side; road way supports.

By not cutting one of the upper beams, you will cause the bridge to twist to the side prior to falling. Removal of debris is thus made more difficult and the reuse of the main girders made impossible.

Do not harbor any great hopes during these very simple bridge demolitions nor any expectations concerning destructive effects. You will only interrupt traffic for a short period of time. In most cases, the enemy, utilizing modern construction methods, will rebuild the bridge destroyed in a relatively short time. As a result it is not as important how you blow a bridge but when you do it. A technically primitive demolition job, executed shortly before decisive operations, is far more important militarily speaking than an outstanding demolition job executed during a slack period when the enemy is not so dependent upon the use of the bridge.

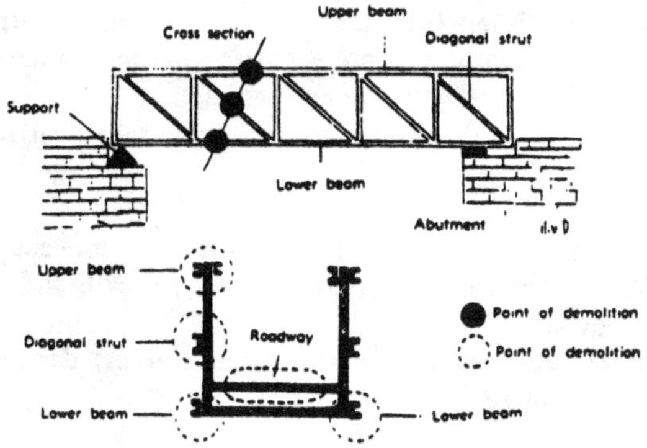

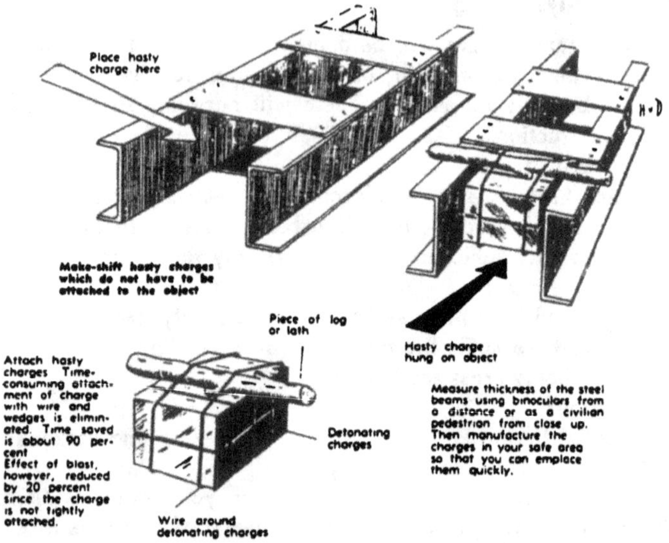

21. Temporary Occupation of Towns by Guerrilla Units

The occupation forces may institute the following measures: dismantling important industrial plants and shipping them out of the country along with the labor force; mass deportation of civilians that are suspected by the occupation forces; large scale destruction of public and industrial installations which cannot be dismantled such as power stations, gas works, railroad installations, bridges, etc.

The enemy will especially implement these measures when he is forced by events which are beyond our sphere of influence (defeats on the front) to withdraw from the territory he has occupied. If guerrilla units and the civilian resistance movement are able to prevent him from doing this, they will render the country invaluable services by preserving at least a portion of the industry and public installations for post-war reconstruction.

In order to do this you must be able to take over towns quickly and efficiently. Do this as follows:

Phase One:

Effect coordination between civilian resistance movement and guerrilla unit. The civilian resistance movement will aid the guerrilla unit as follows:

a. Reconoiter enemy billets, staging areas, depots and strong points in the town.

b. Reconoiter favorable assembly areas (apartments, sewage system) for raiding parties.

c. Find out the best means of infiltration into these assembly areas, i.e., through the sewage system, via back yards, gardens, and parks; smuggling in by vehicles, or moving during blackouts, and by taking advantage of curfew hours.

d. Commanders of raiding parties will conduct a reconnaissance in civilian clothes on their targets; during this operation they will be guided by members of the civilian resistance movement familiar with the area.

Phase Two:

Bring up the guerrilla unit. The resistance movement will point out roads and provide security.

Phase Three:

Raiding parties infiltrate into the town and move into the assembly areas through sewage systems, apartments and shops near the prospective targets.

Phase Four:

The most important targets (see figure) will be attacked suddenly. The main body of the guerrilla unit still outside the town will be brought up by improvised motor transport, if need be, and will eliminate any enemy resistance.

Break down your unit as follows:

Assign detachments to isolate the town by sealing off the main routes of communication at critical points, such as bridges, defiles, etc.

Assign detachments to occupy weak targets or those not defended.

Organize raiding parties to eliminate billets, guards, and strong points.

Security elements should support the raiding parties encountering heavy resistance or oppose enemy reserves.

You have to immediately motorize your security elements. Consequently, motor pools will be included in the most important targets. Assign drivers to the security elements.

Targets:

Occupy bridges as this will guarantee free flow of traffic for us. At the same time, it will block the enemy's lines of communication.

Occupy radio stations as this allows us to broadcast announcements to our own population and communicate with friendly foreign nations.

Occupy administrative and government buildings when enemy no longer offers unified and coordinated defense. This will facilitate control of our population; secure archives and documents and assist in arresting important collaborators and high enemy officials.

Occupation of prisons will prevent the political police from executing political prisoners.

Occupy telephone switchboards and administrative buildings to prevent the enemy from using them. Telephone communication system can only be interrupted suddenly at a central point.

Occupy railroad installations to prevent the enemy from retreating with his heavy material. This also prevents the rapid arrival of outside reinforcements. Due to lack of personnel you may have to be content with blocking the main routes of communications.

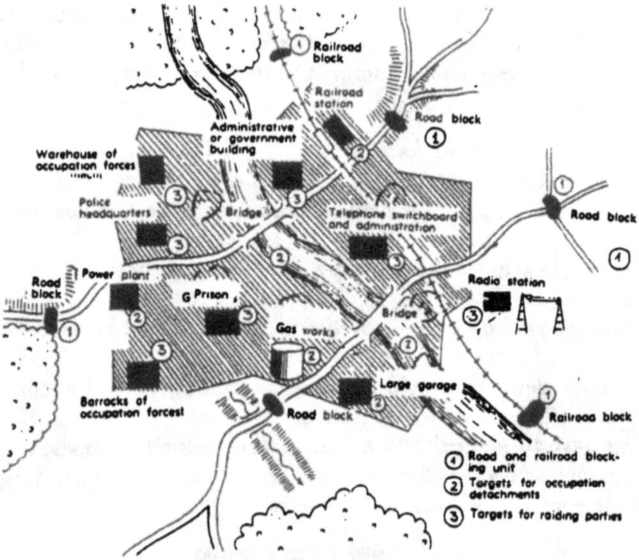

IV. How an Enemy with Modern Equipment Will Operate Against your Guerrilla Detachmnt

In order to be successful in counter guerrilla warfare in the long run, he is forced to occupy all important points simultaneously at all times, and at the same time systematically clear territories infested with guerrilla units.

In order to control roads he will utilize motorized, mechanized or armored raiding units. The intermediate area will be controlled by helicopters.

A detailed and never ending reconnaissance is important.

Considerable commitment of personnel (infantry) is thus inevitable. This is one reason why highly mechanized armies, where the percentage of infantry personnel is very small, have such a great difficulty in suppressing guerrilla operations.

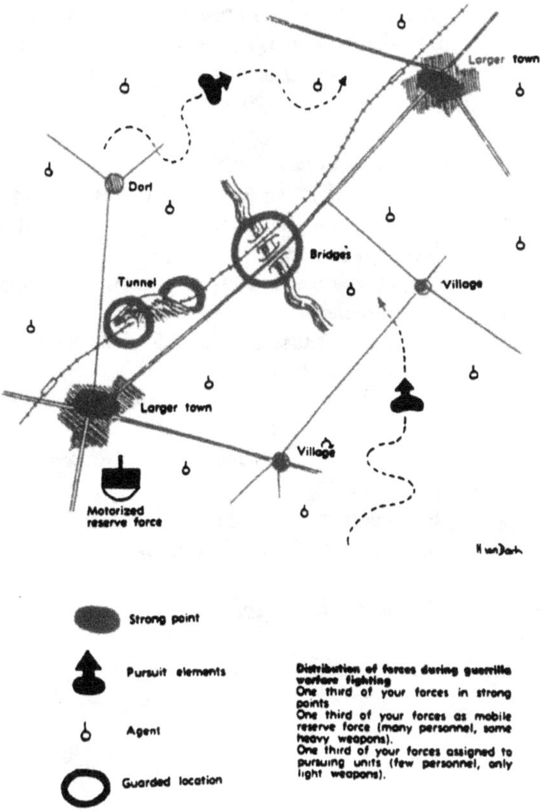

Direct commitment of the air force is normally too costly in comparison to the results obtained (except helicopter or airborne operations).

During local resistance, company strong points are placed 10 km. apart.

Long-range radio equipment as a standard item of issue is necessary for troops. Normally, this will result in a difference of one echelon (i.e., the platoon will need the radio equipment of the company, the company that of the battalion, etc.).

Supply requirements are small since only a few small encounters will take place. Support elements will have to be escorted at all times.

Billets will be installed in larger, interconnected buildings. They will be protected by barbed wire and machine gun and mortar emplacements as well as by searchlights. By means of such fortification, more personnel can be allocated to pursuit units.

Road traffic will only be authorized during daytime. At road junctions or intersections all vehicles will be stopped, convoys will be formed and accompanied through areas infested by guerrillas. Two escort vehicles (light tanks, armored scout cars) will accompany approximately 25 vehicles.

Organization and Operation of Pursuit Units

Pursuit units are composed of 20 to 25 men (platoon) and only carry light weapons with them, i.e., submachine gun, assault gun, light machine gun, and hand grenades.

Each unit has the mission to hunt a certain guerrilla detachment for days or, if necessary, for weeks.

To do this effectively, the unit must conceal all of its movements, live the same as a guerrilla detachment.

By your own actions it will become inevitable that the presence of the guerrilla detachment will be given away.

Enemy agents equipped with radios localize the area in which your detachment must operate.

Observation helicopters keep in touch once your detachment has been discovered and direct the pursuit unit from the air to the area of operation.

Airborne reserves will be brought up.

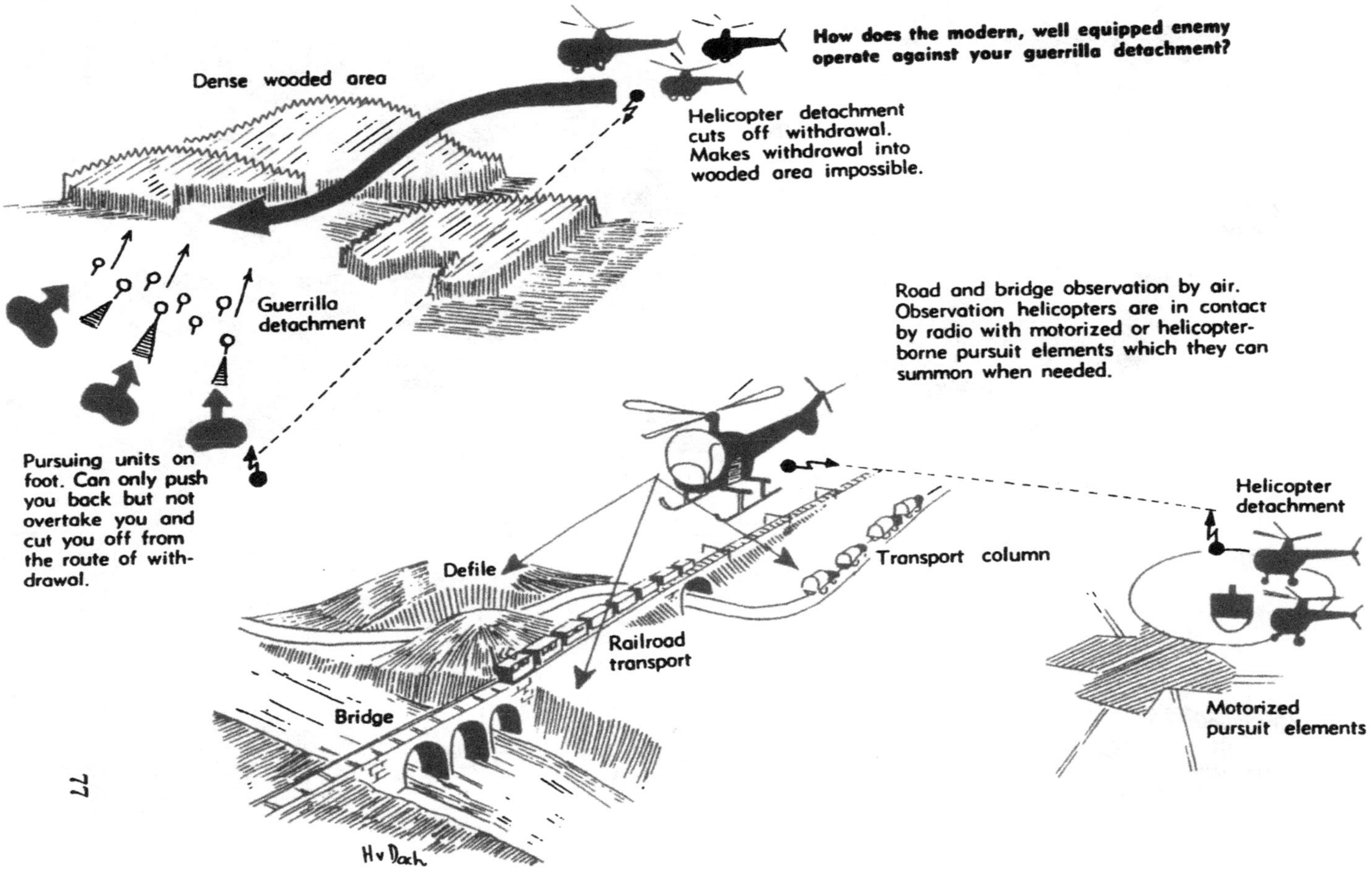
How does the modern, well equipped enemy operate against your guerrilla detachment?
Dense wooded area
Helicopter detachment cuts off withdrawal. Makes withdrawal into wooded area impossible.
Guerrilla detachment
Pursuing units on foot. Can only push you back but not overtake you and cut you off from the route of withdrawal.
Road and bridge observation by air. Observation helicopters are in contact by radio with motorized or helicopter-borne pursuit elements which they can summon when needed.
Helicopter detachment
Transport column
Defile
Railroad transport
Bridge
Motorized pursuit elements
H v Dach

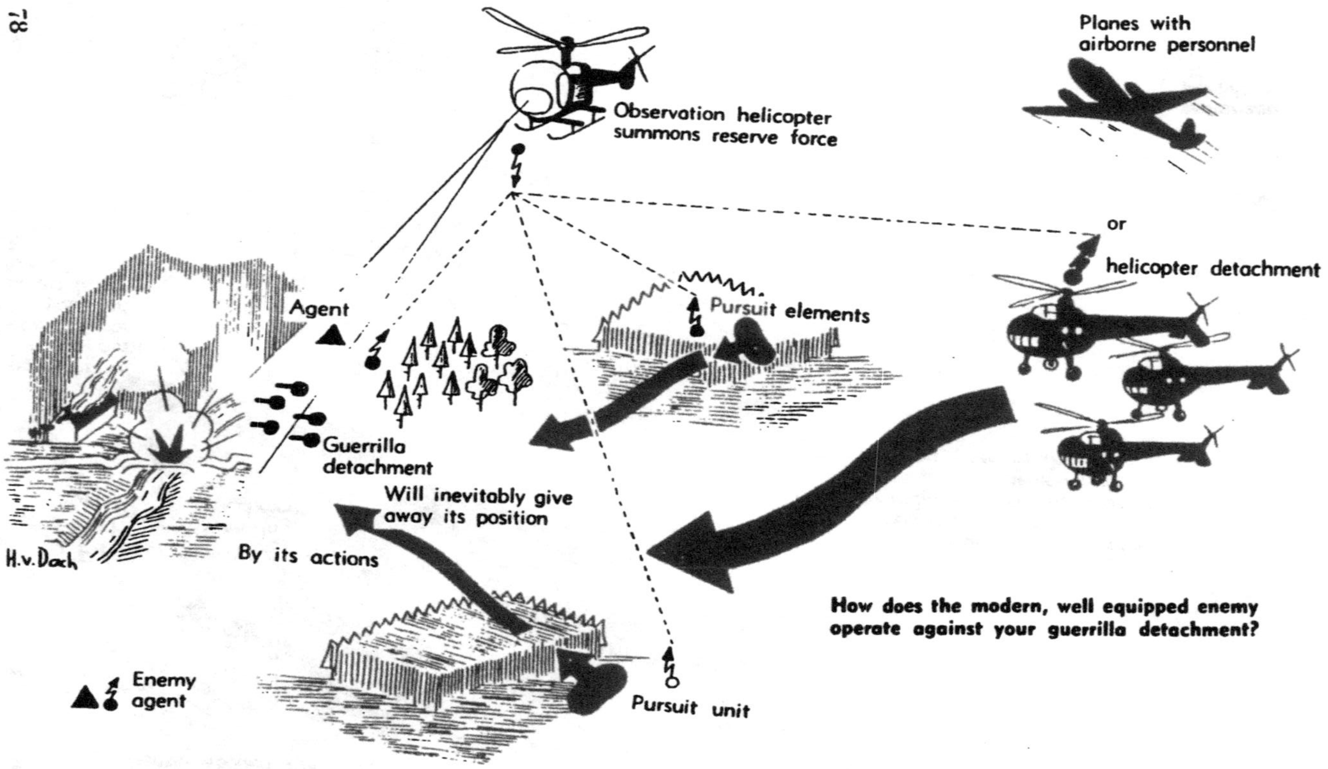

How does the modern, well equipped enemy operate against your guerrilla detachment?

Mopping-up Operations by Larger Units

A thin line of infantry will comb through the guerrilla infested area on foot and on a wide front. Sector for a company is normally 3 kilometers.

At a sufficient distance a motorized reserve force—reinforced company—will follow.

If artillery and armor are available, they will be assigned to the reserve force.

If the infantry encounters strong resistance the reserve force will be called in by radio..

Since a counter-guerrilla operation of this type only forces the guerrillas to withdraw but does not cause their destruction, a blocking force against which the enemy is driven, has to be established prior to commencement of the operation. Usually, the blocking force will be stationed along some impassable terrain feature such as a river or mountain range.

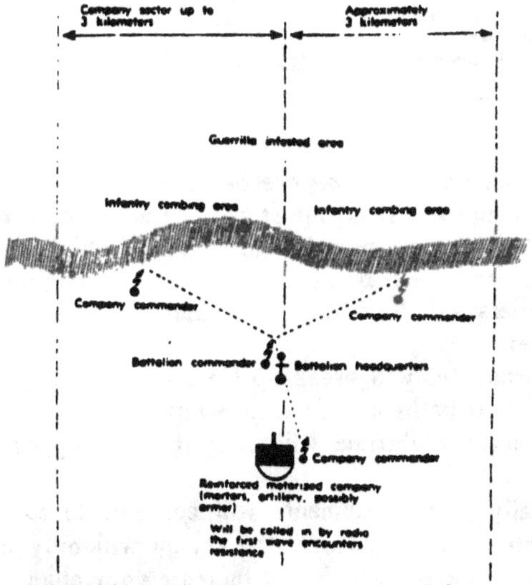

Organization of mopping-up operations

Good observation and fields of fire are the prerequisites for positioning a "net":

Approximate assignment of forces is as follows:

"Net":	One fourth of the infantry personnel available
	Two thirds of heavy weapons available
"Beaters":	Three fourths of available infantry personnel
	One third of heavy weapons available

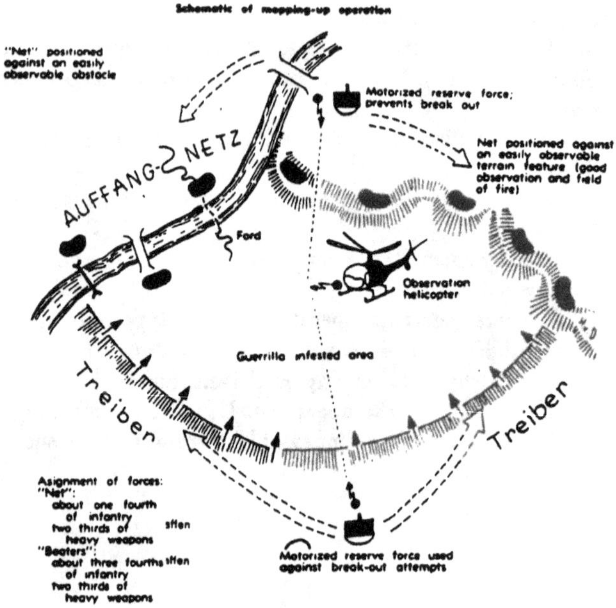

Hints for a break-out when you are being hunted

Do not attempt to break out at the beginning of a mopping-up operation since the enemy morale and strength is high.

Later, the enemy will be more careless, more negligent and less attentive. Soldiers will tend to bypass more difficult and tiresome terrain features.

Linear formations will break up since people prefer—especially at night—to follow paths and favorable terrain features out of laziness. Consequently, nighttime will offer the best opportunities for escape.

Occasionally pursuit elements will concentrate to eat and to reorganize. During these periods, the enemy will only have a thin screen of security guards which will increase your chances of breaking out.

In order to pursue a guerrilla detachment of only 100 men, the enemy will soon need a force ten to twenty times larger—one to two battalions.

After a successful break-out assemble at a pre-designated rally point and move as fast and far as possible from the area.

How you can evade an enemy mopping-up operation

Attempt to sneak through or break through the encirclement

If this is impossible, occupy well camouflaged hideouts. The enemy may not notice you.

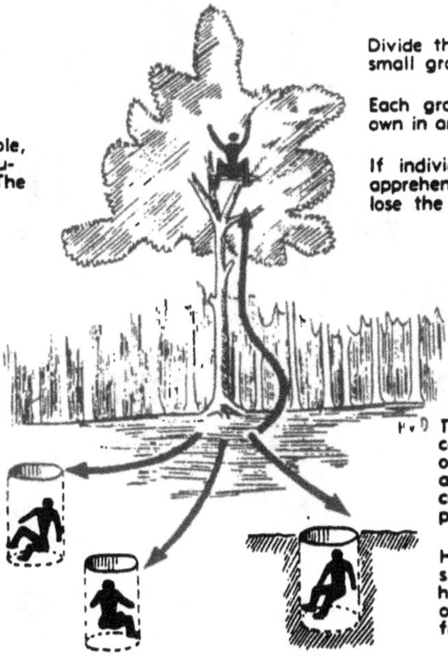

Divide the entire unit into small groups of 3 to 4 men.

Each group will hide on its own in an area assigned to it.

If individual groups are apprehended you will not lose the entire unit.

The group leader will camouflage the holes of his team members and then occupy a concealed position possibly in a tree.

He will also give the signal when danger has passed, and everyone may emerge from concealment.

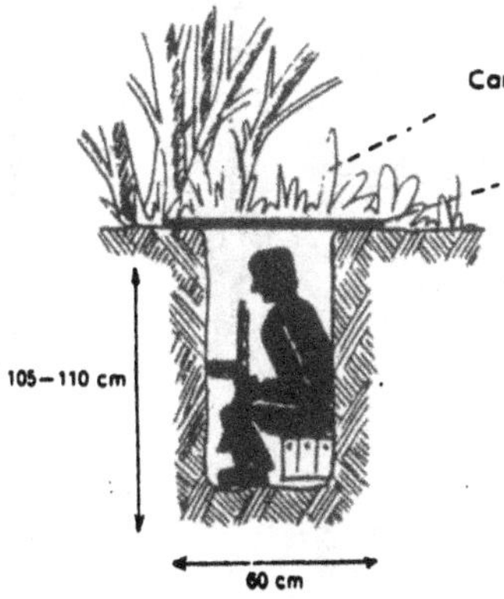

Camouflage—sod, leaves, etc.

Support for camouflage cover—lath frame, log frame, with sacking or shelter half on top.

You may reduce the possibility of enemy search elements stepping on the camouflage cover, breaking into the hole and discovering your people, by digging holes halfway under bushes, hazel trees, tree trunkc, etc.

If the enemy does not use dogs you have a good chance of remaining undetected. Consequently, during fire fights, concentrate your fire on dogs and their handlers. They are among your greatest enemies. Once a hole has been discovered, all other members of the group throw off their camouflage and engage in the fire fight, for the enemy will conduct a thorough search of the area.

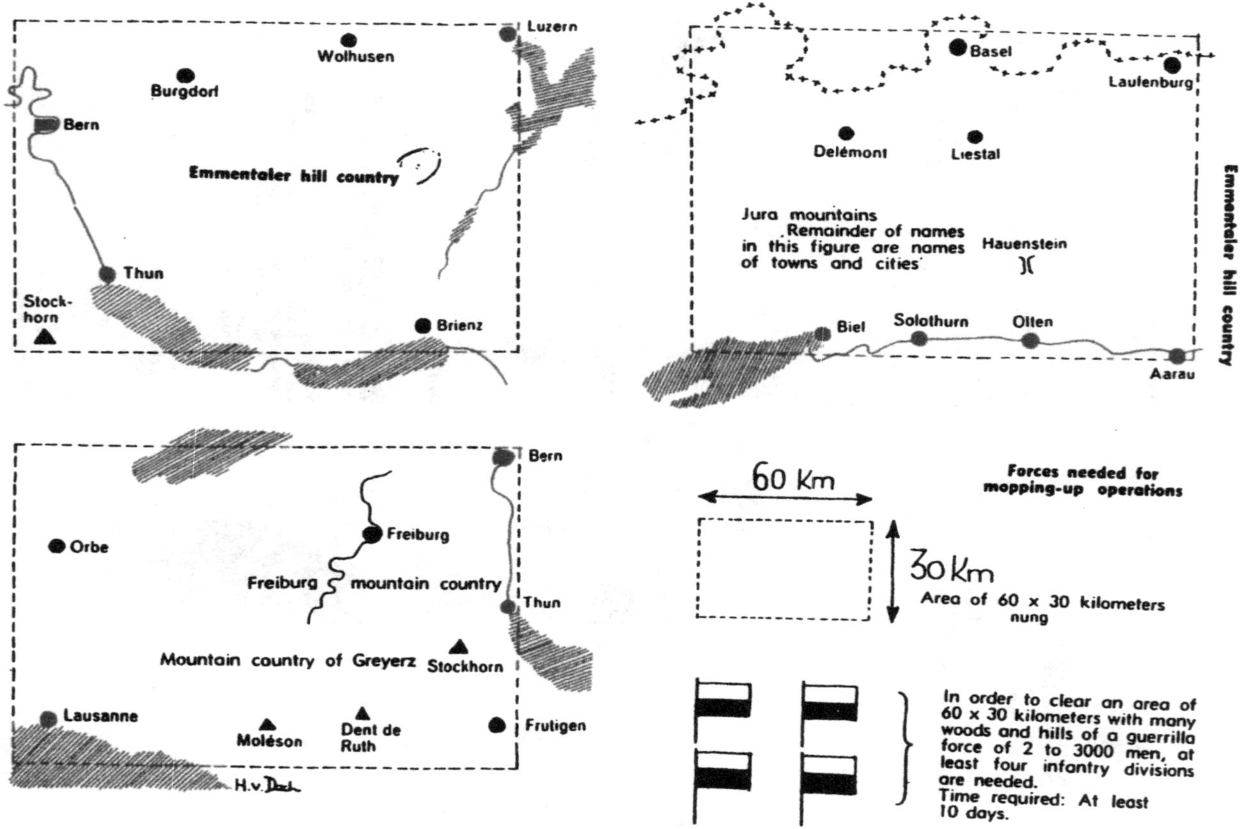
Luzern
Wolhusen
Burgdorf
Bern
Emmentaler hill country
Thun
Stock-
horn
Brienz
Basel
Laufenburg
Delémont
Liestal
Jura mountains
Remainder of names
in this figure are names
of towns and cities
Hauenstein
Biel
Solothurn
Olten
Aarau
Emmentaler hill country
Bern
Orbe
Freiburg
Freiburg mountain country
Thun
Mountain country of Greyerz
Stockhorn
Lausanne
Moléson
Dent de
Ruth
Frutigen
H.v.Dach
60 Km
30 Km
Area of 60 x 30 kilometers
nung
Forces needed for
mopping-up operations
In order to clear an area of 60 x 30 kilometers with many woods and hills of a guerrilla force of 2 to 3000 men, at least four infantry divisions are needed.
Time required: At least 10 days.

Part II

Organization and Operation of the Civilian Resistance Movement

I. Organization

1. Missions of the Civilian Resistance Movement

a. Maintain belief in final victory.

b. Inform the population concerning appropriate behavior toward the enemy.

c. Collect and conceal weapons and ammunition for the moment when, together with the guerrilla units, an open uprising can be staged. This will usually coincide with the approaching collapse of the enemy, or approach of allied troops.

d. Develop an intelligence service which will assist guerrilla units, and portions of the Army still holding out as well as allied foreign countries.

e. Maintain a list of all atrocities committed by each official of the oppressors for the "Day for Settling Accounts." (Through posters, leaflets and rumors, you have to make sure that everybody, even the enemy, knows about this. This knowledge will keep many an official from committing himself).

f. Publish a free newspaper ("underground paper").

g. Broadcast radio programs ("Freedom transmitter").

h. Establish an organization to hide persons sought by the enemy police (State Security Service).

i. Establish an escape and evasion net for crew members of downed airplanes of allied countries or for escaped prisoners. (Refer these people to our own guerrilla units.)

j. Falsify ration cards for the supply of persons expelled from the community as so-called "state enemies" and sentenced by the enemy to a "slow death."

k. Counterfeit money and identification papers for persons mentioned above as well as those that had to "disappear" because of the State Security Service.

l. Fight against collaboration (cooperation with the enemy).

m. Organize sabotage. Organize attempts against the lives of especially cruel officials of the enemy as well as prominent traitors.

n. Organize fighting elements for the time of open uprising.

Curve of Collaboration

A very small percentage of the population will collaborate with the enemy. This percentage will increase sharply right after the implementation of terrorist measures; it will then remain constant and after a while will decrease.

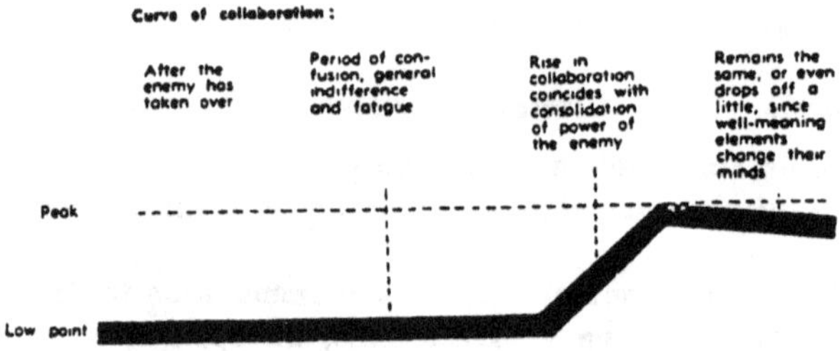

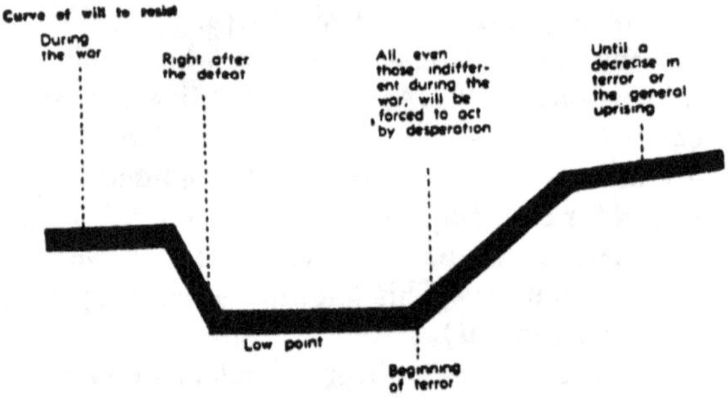

The population is prepared for collaboration with the resistance movement by the mistakes of the occupation power and its "Quisling government." Some of these mistakes are: forced conscription of labor forces for abroad; excessive work quotas ("production quotas"); breach of promise, blackmail, arrests, hostages, torture, deportation, firing squads; forced requisitions, dismantling of plants; overbearing behavior.

2. Recruiting for the Resistance Movement

In spite of all their good intentions, not all people are suitable for active participation in the resistance movement.

You have to select carefully active resistance members from among the masses available.

The success or failure of the resistance movement depends upon this selection.

People that have held public positions during peace time should not be recruited for the resistance movement. It is likely that these individuals will be arrested and subjected to brain washing. They should have no knowledge of the resistance movement, so your organization will not be compromised, nor lose members.

Make sure that this "basic rule of recruitment" is well known, even to the enemy. Thus you can protect these valuable and courageous people to some degree since once the enemy is aware of this policy, his interest in them will diminish.

Examples of members unsuitable for the resistance movement are: prominent politicians both active or retired; leading economists, editors, professors, important administration officials.

All these persons are too well known to participate in the "underground movement." They certainly will be shadowed, will be arrested sooner or later, or even executed. For them it is best to join guerrilla units.

Anybody wishing to work with the resistance movement must be as inconspicuous as possible and remain silent in public.

Prominent personalities are also exposed to one special type of danger. During the early phase of the occupation they may be forced publically to support the enemy.

3. Joining a Guerrilla Detachment or Changing Over to the Resistance Movement

Personal danger in the "fight of ideologies" is no longer measured in terms of whether you belong to the resistance movement or not. If, by virtue of profession or descent, you belong to a walk of life looked upon unfavorably by the enemy, he will liquidate you sooner or later either by deportation or by execution. To remain a "non-participant" in the resistance movement is no longer useful since the system of arresting hostages or mass deportation will indiscriminately be applied to everyone, fighter or non-fighter.

In the hour of distress nobody will help the "non-fighter." As a member of the resistance movement you are protected by it. It can warn you when the enemy intends to arrest you and help you escape.

All those who by nature of their descent, profession or ideology are considered potential enemies and thus risk deportation or executive, had best immediately join a guerrilla detachment or the resistance movement.

Contact and work with individuals of similar conviction. If one remains alone and isolated his morale will deteriorate. The isolated member of the resistance is subject to the same threat of fear and desperation that a soldier may feel when isolated from his unit during conventional warfare.

Organization of a cell
(ideal case, principle sketch)

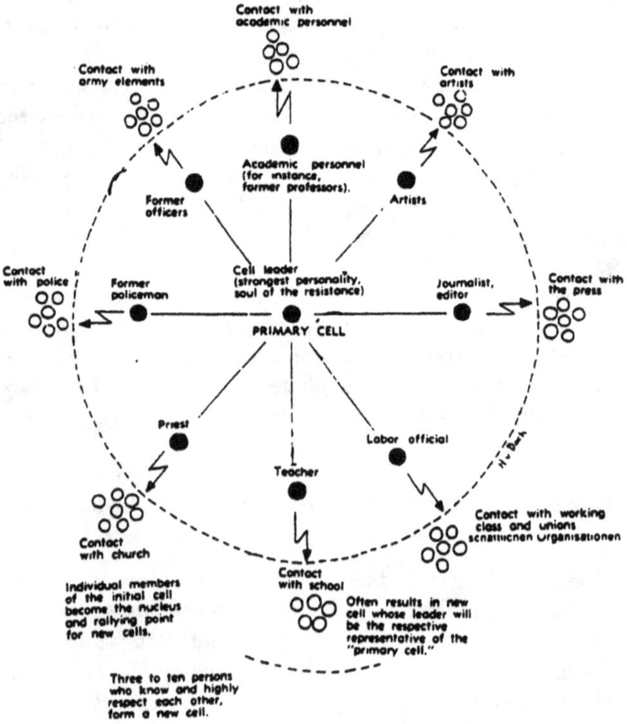

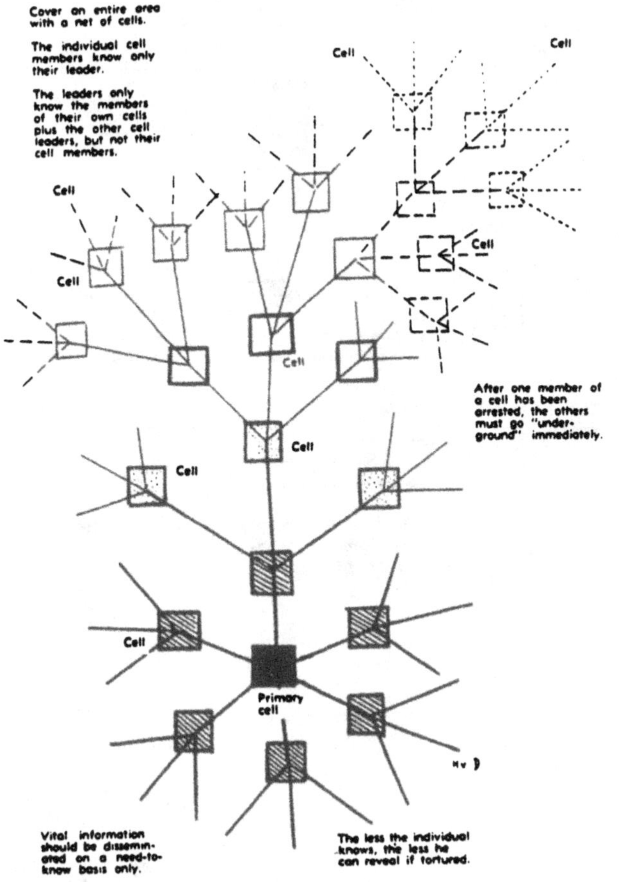

4. Activities of the Various Sections

a. Information and propaganda section informs the population on:

(1) General behavior
(2) Behavior during police interrogation
(3) Behavior after police interrogation
(4) Behavior in prison, during deportation and in forced labor camps.

b. Information service

Disseminates news about the true war situation.

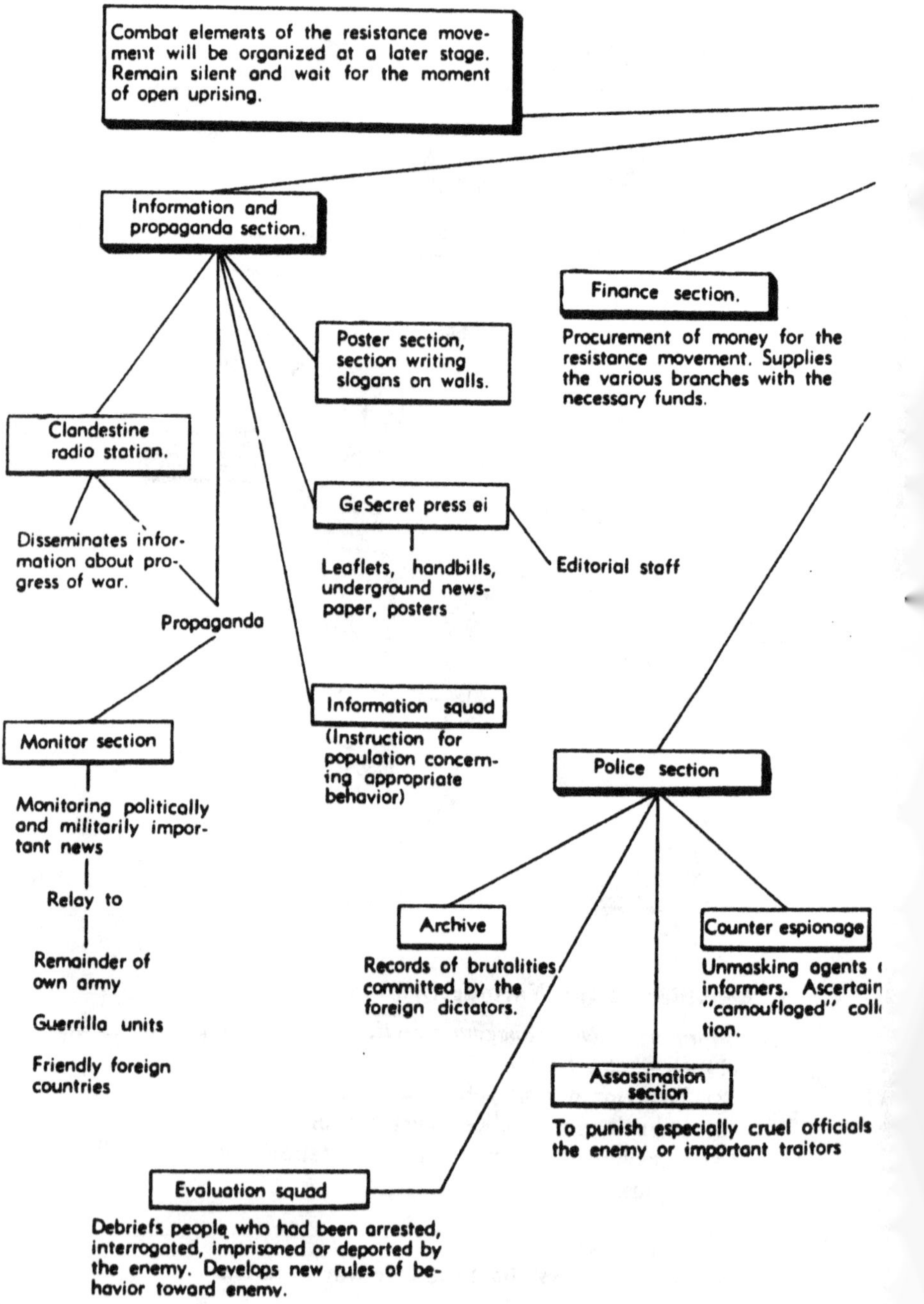

Combat elements of the resistance movement will be organized at a later stage. Remain silent and wait for the moment of open uprising.
Information and propaganda section.
Finance section.
Procurement of money for the resistance movement. Supplies the various branches with the necessary funds.
Poster section, section writing slogans on walls.
Clandestine radio station.
Disseminates information about progress of war.
Propaganda
GeSecret press ei
Leaflets, handbills, underground newspaper, posters
Editorial staff
Monitor section
Monitoring politically and militarily important news
Relay to
Remainder of own army
Guerrilla units
Friendly foreign countries
Information squad
(Instruction for population concerning appropriate behavior)
Police section
Archive
Records of brutalities committed by the foreign dictators.
Counter espionage
Unmasking agents
informers. Ascertain
"camouflaged" coll
tion.
Assassination section
To punish especially cruel officials
the enemy or important traitors
Evaluation squad
Debriefs people who had been arrested, interrogated, imprisoned or deported by the enemy. Develops new rules of behavior toward enemy.

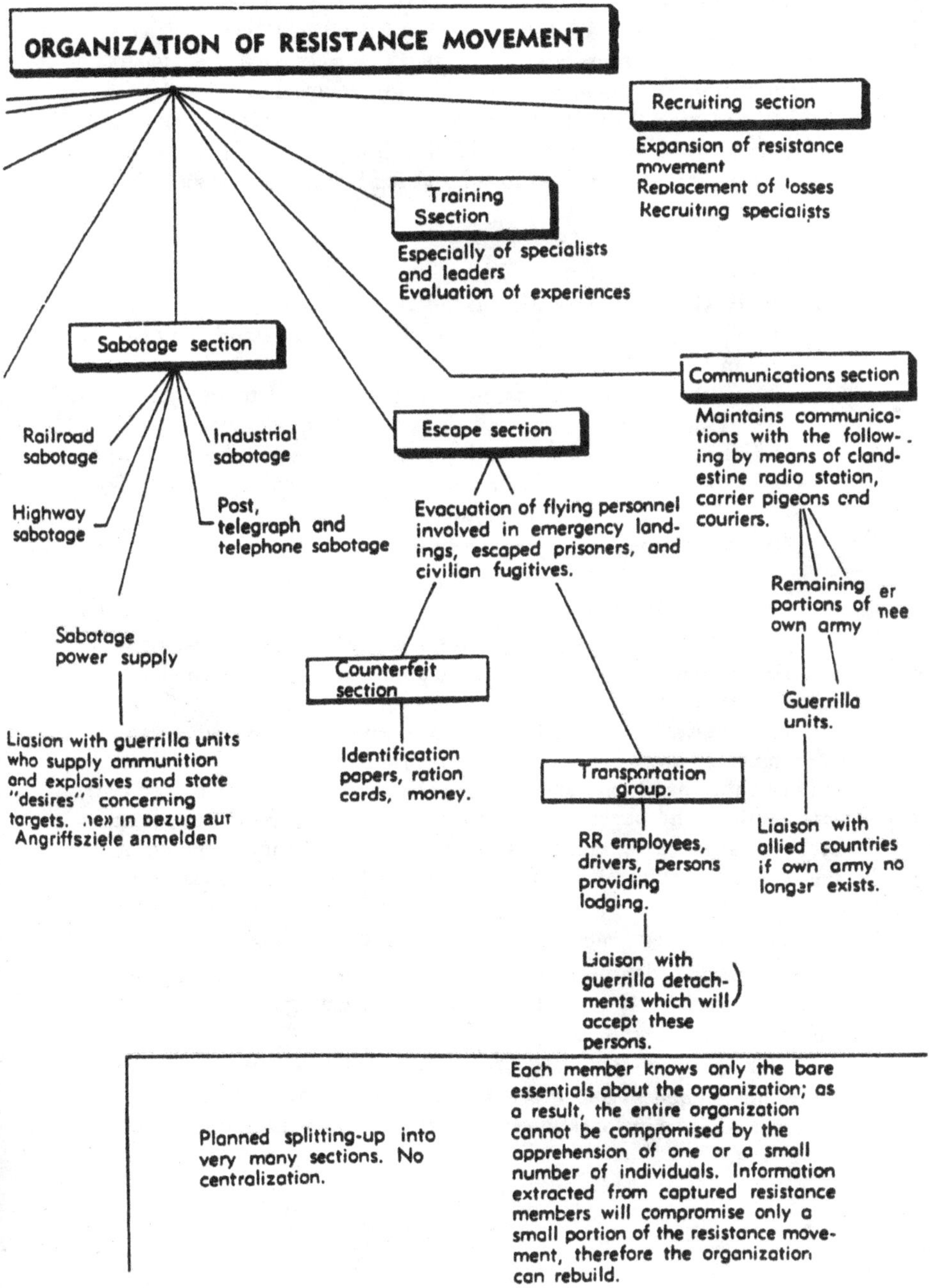
ORGANIZATION OF RESISTANCE MOVEMENT
Recruiting section
Expansion of resistance movement
Replacement of losses
Recruiting specialists
Training Ssection
Especially of specialists and leaders
Evaluation of experiences
Sabotage section
Communications section
Maintains communications with the following by means of clandestine radio station, carrier pigeons and couriers.
Railroad sabotage
Industrial sabotage
Escape section
Highway sabotage
Post, telegraph and telephone sabotage
Evacuation of flying personnel involved in emergency landings, escaped prisoners, and civilian fugitives.
Remaining portions of own army
Sabotage power supply
Counterfeit section
Guerrilla units.
Liasion with guerrilla units who supply ammunition and explosives and state "desires" concerning targets.
Identification papers, ration cards, money.
Transportation group.
Liaison with allied countries if own army no longer exists.
RR employees, drivers, persons providing lodging.
Liaison with guerrilla detachments which will accept these persons.
Planned splitting-up into very many sections. No centralization.
Each member knows only the bare essentials about the organization; as a result, the entire organization cannot be compromised by the apprehension of one or a small number of individuals. Information extracted from captured resistance members will compromise only a small portion of the resistance movement, therefore the organization can rebuild.

c. *Organization of "Escape Section" (20 to 30 Persons)*

Take care of the displacement of escapees: (1) A few drivers from cross-country transportation firms; (2) A few RR dispatchers and conductors and engineers who will allow escapees to ride without a ticket and hide them from enemy security units on the trains, if necessary; (3) A number of reliable inhabitants maintain relay stations, where escapees can be lodged and fed before, during and after transport.

d. *Finance section*

Funds will be procured in the following manner:

(1) Counterfeit money printed in allied countries and smuggled in to us.
(2) Counterfeit money printed in the occupied territory.
(3) "Camouflaged" support funds with large companies.
(4) Recruiting of bank and postal employees, who will go "underground" with the resistance movement at a favorable moment and with large sums.
(5) Raids upon enemy finance offices.

Utilization of money:

This money will be used to fund espionage operations, bribe officials, provide for persons that have gone "underground" and support the resistance press.

It is desirable to establish a compensation fund. He who wants to or must go underground must be assured that his family will not have to suffer more than absolutely necessary. By means of monetary contributions and payments in kind these families must be supported by the resistance movement. The same kind of support should be available to families of deported, imprisoned and executed persons.

e. *Organization of counterfeit group (8 to 10 specialists)*

Counterfeit identification papers and change those in use. (Passports, ID cards, ration cards, counterfeit money, gasoline coupons, official stamps, tickets, etc.).

This group is composed of the owner of a printing shop who makes his equipment and material available; a section to counterfeit rubber stamps; mimeograph section; and a liaison man to resistance movement.

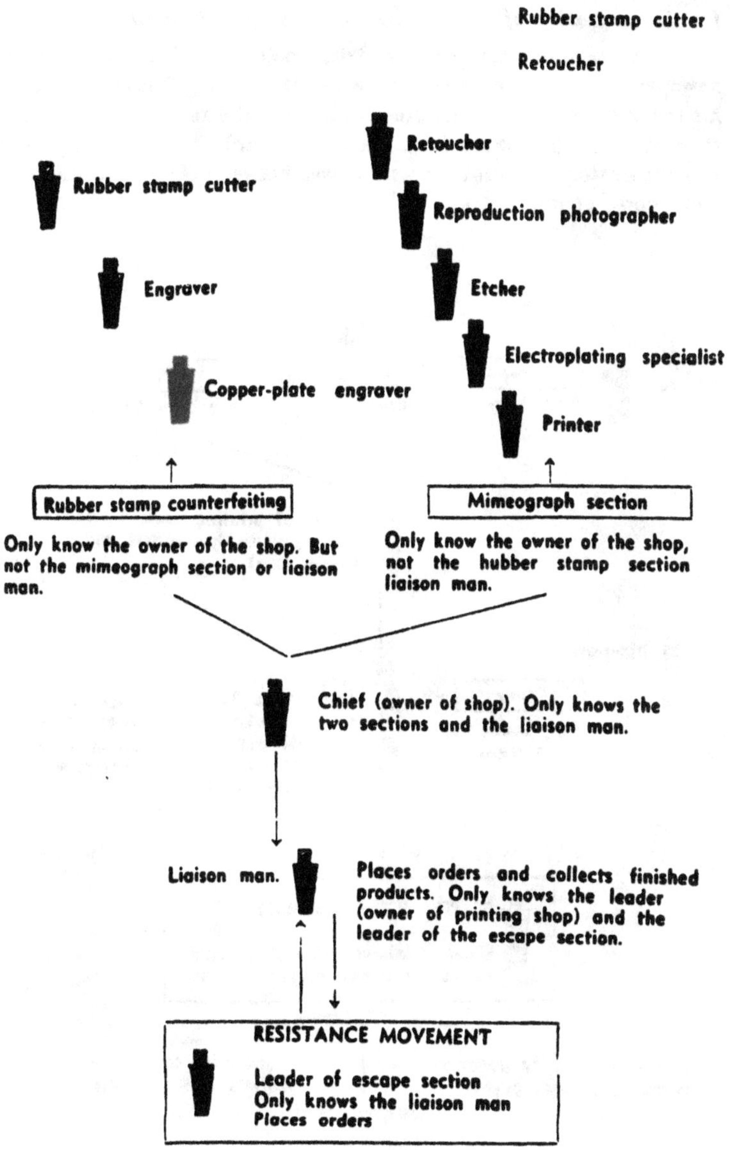
Rubber stamp cutter
Retoucher
Retoucher
Rubber stamp cutter
Reproduction photographer
Engraver
Etcher
Electroplating specialist
Copper-plate engraver
Printer
Rubber stamp counterfeiting
Mimeograph section
Only know the owner of the shop. But not the mimeograph section or liaison man.
Only know the owner of the shop, not the hubber stamp section liaison man.
Chief (owner of shop). Only knows the two sections and the liaison man.
Liaison man.
Places orders and collects finished products. Only knows the leader (owner of printing shop) and the leader of the escape section.
RESISTANCE MOVEMENT
Leader of escape section
Only knows the liaison man
Places orders

f. Organization of secret printing press (5 to 6 men)

This section will print leaflets, posters, and an underground newspaper. It is composed of: owner of printing house who makes his machinery and installations available to the resistance movement; at least two type setters (one machine setter); two printers; editor and illustrator; liaison man who moves between the resistance movement and "counterfeit group."

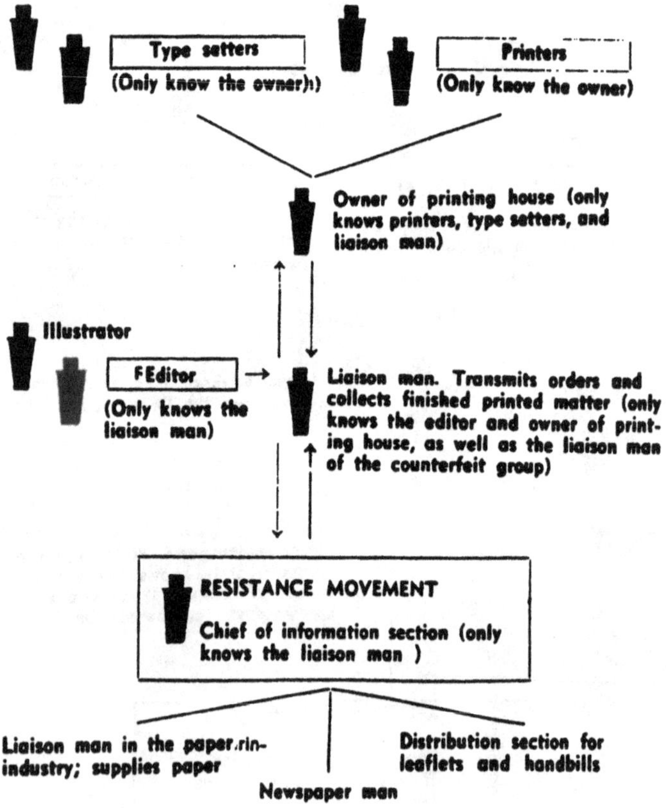

g. Section responsible for writing slogans on walls

Material needed includes; paint buckets, large paint brushes, sneakers or tennis shoes, bicycles (make no noise and are relatively fast) and pistols for security elements.

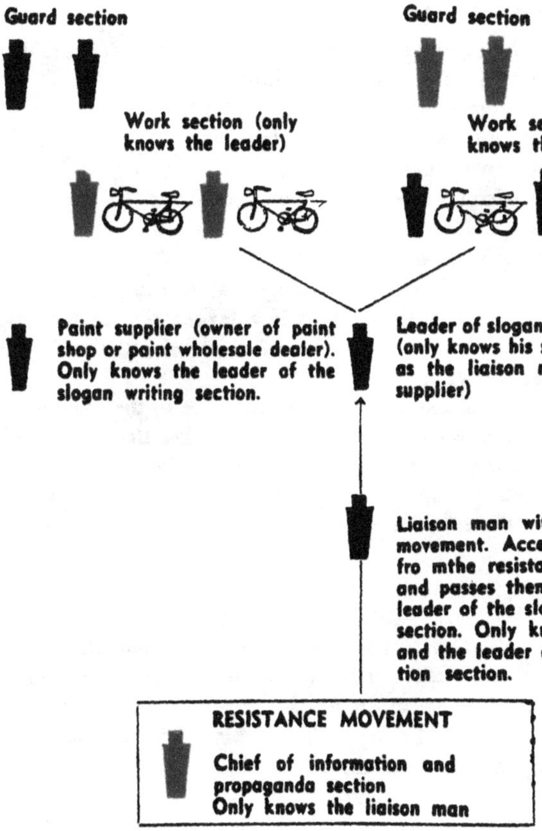

II. Enemy Operations

1. Basic Rules of Terror

If you resist political indoctrination and the enemy realizes that he is failing in his attempts to "convert" you to his ideology, he will attempt to obtain obedience through fear. He will try to create this fear by terror. The enemy has developed terror techniques which have proved very effective. You therefore must be prepared. If you are acquainted with these techniques you can resist them more easily.

These terror measures are:

a. Surveillance of telephone and letters through censorship;
b. Establishment of an agent and informer net;
c. Arbitrary arrests;
d. No public trials except "show trials";
e. Arbitrary sentences;
f. Lengthy prison sentences out of proportion to the offense.

Surveillance of telephone and letters

The chances of success of the enemy mail censorship and telephone surveillance are practically zero in a larger city such as Bern where 160,000 telephone conversations are made and 200,000 pieces of mail are posted daily.

Long conversations are especially of nuisance to the enemy since he can only monitor a few conversations or he takes the risk of missing something important by stopping too early.

Harmless paraphrasing and simple code words during telephone conversations and in letters even further reduce the effectiveness of enemy censorship.

Arbitrary arrests

The enemy will arbitrarily arrest completely harmless people in order to spread the rumor that they have become victims of his surveillance net. He wants to create the impression that his net is closely knit and effective. Do not fall for this trick but make some estimate of its capabilities and limitations.

Arbitrary sentences

The enemy does not punish according to the law but according to political requirements. As a result seldom is the same sentence decreed for the same offense. Thus, you always have to expect the worst. You may be sent to a forced labor camp for an indeterminate period or even executed for the slightest offense, if you are unlucky enough to be apprehended at a politically unfavorable moment. Expedience dictates enemy action.

Brutal behavior during arrests and interrogations

Night arrests increase the sense of terror. People can no longer sleep in peace. Brutal treatment during interrogations and in the prisons tends to surround the State Security Service and its institutions (interrogation cellars, prisons, etc.) with a cloak of horror.

Relatively high sentences

He who only writes a slogan on a wall runs the risk of deportation to a uranium mine just the same as the radio operator of a clandestine radio station. He who only throws a handful of sand into the grease box of a railroad car runs the risk of being shot the same as the one who sets fire to a large garage or even destroys a transformer station.

Propagation of "horror," however, is a two-edged sword. Used adroitly, it can serve your cause by mobilizing, through hate and desperation, those that have remained passive until now. Do not attempt to mobilize the "undecided" by "counterterror." Be patient; the enemy will take such measures that with the passage of time they will come to you quite automatically. Individuals forced to join you under pressure are unreliable. If needed, these people can still be used in the regular army where they have a close relationship with others and are under permanent control. However, during the resistance fight, where everything depends upon the secrecy and steadfastness of the individual, they are of no use, and even constitute a danger.

2. State Security Service (Political Police such as the "Ochrana," "Gestapo," "Cheka," "GPU," "SD," and "AVO.")

The first prerequisite to be able to fight the enemy without suffering undue loss is to know him.

The State Security Service (political police) is a foreign and sinister thing to you. For this reason it will present a greater danger than the actual occupation troops who are individuals much like ourselves and whose reactions you can estimate and predict.

Actually, the State Security Service is less a police organization than a terror organization. Their knowledge of police techniques is slight and never equal those of a normal security police or a criminal investigation organization.

The actions of the political police are thus rough and do not demonstrate any finesse. What they lack in technical ability they compensate for by increased brutality and cruelty.

The political police do not have a tight organization like the military. It is rather a mixture, hard to define at that, between "Party-Military," "Normal Police," and "Criminal Investigation Police."

The real striking power in any of these sectors is naturally small. The secrecy, however, increases the effects of terror. The State Security Service exists less on effective results than on a reputation of terror.

Normally the enemy does not even know himself exactly where the area of responsibility of the State Security Service begins and where it ends. His natural tendency to create a state within the state is thus great and mostly successful. As a rule, he also tends to terrorize his own army and administrative officials. Consequently, there is in most cases no real cooperation between these offices but only a latent tension and rivalry which in turn reduces mutual effectiveness.

Members of the State Security Service normally work in civilian clothes. They appear in uniform only on special occasions.

The State Security Service is not bound by firm rules and laws. In contrast to the normal police it has no intention of acting in a preventive capacity by its mere presence or to find culprits, if necessary, but rather it operates on the principle that "to prevent is better than to heal." This means: each person who might become a potential enemy is liquidated now as a preventive measure, in many cases even before he has committed himself against the occupying power. For this reason entire sections of the population or professional groups rather than just specific individuals are systematically eliminated.

The constant distrust even of their own officials is not caused by the profession as such, but is part of the system. By involving many agencies even during small affairs, no official can deviate from the line. Each must attempt to surpass automatically his colleagues in "cruelty," "faithfulness to the system," and "hate toward the enemy." As a result everyone is watching each other.

3. The Struggle for the Youth

A. General

An occupation may last many years. The enemy and especially

the "Quisling" government installed by him, to consolidate power, will attempt to subvert the minds of the youth.

The enemy not only wants to exploit economically and militarily the occupied territory for his own war purposes, but also wants to incorporate it into his ideological sphere of power. As a consequence, you are not only to be conquered but also, if possible, to be converted. With this policy, he not only hopes to obtain labor forces but also eventually individuals who will support his ideology.

The enemy will write off the older generation, at least partially, as being impossible to convert. He will rely on terror to keep them in check and eliminate them, if necessary, by deportation or execution.

He will, however, turn with increased vigor toward the youth which he will attempt to convert by a variety of means—from promises to naked threats.

The struggle for youth is roughly divided into two parts:

(1) Suppressing the traditional youth organizations and replacing them by a "State Youth Movement."

(2) Elimination or at least a great reduction of the influence of family, church, and school upon young people, and replacing it with the influence of the party and its youth organizations.

B. Suppression of free youth organizations

The enemy fears the forces of community alive in free youth movement. His demand upon your mind is complete. As a result he cannot tolerate any other youth organizations besides the "State Youth Movement" created by him. Any type of allegiance to the old organizations will not be tolerated.

Specifically, the enemy will forbid the traditional youth organizations to do the following:

(1) Wearing of uniforms or pieces of clothing resembling uniforms;

(2) Displaying insignias, flags, and pennants;

(3) Marching, hiking, camping, etc.;

(4) Participating in any kind of sports activity.

In addition to these active measures of fighting the organizations, strong pressure will be created simultaneously to join the newly created "State Youth Movement." It will be announced, for instance, that in the future any applicant for any type of advanced or key position will be accepted only if he can prove that he was a member of the "State Youth Movement."

Elimination of conventional influence upon youth

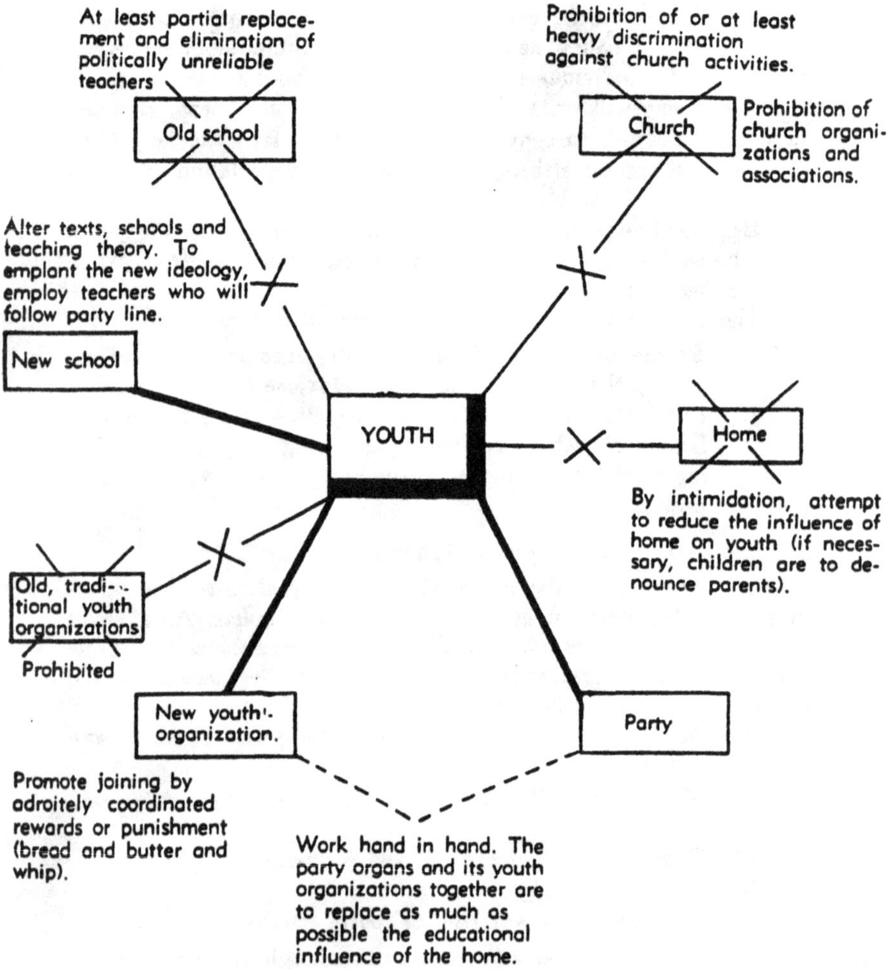

C. Means used by the enemy to exploit the youth include the unscrupulous, diabolic exploitation of:

(1) the youthful desire for action and adventure;
(2) the ability for enthusiasm (phony ideas);
(3) the ability to become easily impressed with such things as flags, uniforms, music, and pictures;
(4) the little developed ability to judge critically;
(5) the fact that youth forgets easily and is resilient;
(6) the "conflict between generations" (normal latent tension with older generation);
(7) the "golden promises" of the future;
(8) the veiled and indirect coercion which is only used as a last resort.

The enemy thus attempts to make the aims of youth the same as his.

First phase of subverting the youth

First of all, the youth is to be enlisted and won over to the enemy's side by subjects of interest to them:

Exploiting the "motor fad" of youth (knowledge of motors, driver's school for motorcycles or cars).

Exploitation of the "hunger for beauty" of youth (films and trips and colorful meetings).

Second phase

Introduction of political lessons (political influence). For the time being, only a very few lessons will be introduced which will go almost unnoticed in the clever, interesting, and technical programs presented by the state. Gradually, the number of hours of political instruction increases until it becomes the main subject.

In conjunction with the above, a slow, almost imperceptible change of emphasis from sports to a systematic pre-military training occurs.

Since occupation may well last many years, there is a great danger of politically poisoning the youth. The enemy places great emphasis on political matters even in wartime.

4. Fighting the Church

A. Enemy operations against the church

The totalitarian enemy will always label the church as a potential "enemy" and will fight it accordingly. He will proceed with the greatest of cunning and will implement the dechristianization of life in stages so as not to be too conspicuous. He will not destroy the church in one attempt but will undermine it slowly over a period of several years. If he proceeds too quickly, general resistance would result.

Under the concept of "church" one must include the Catholic church, reformation church, and independent religious movements (i.e., Methodist church, Christian Science, Jehova's Witnesses, etc.).

Operations against the church will take approximately the following form: (1) slandering the church; (2) making the church an object of ridicule.

In an effort to prevent creation of martyrs, if at all possible, he will attempt to portray church figures as common criminals. For instance, morals charges will be brought against priests or they will be accused of misdemeanors such as embezzlement.

B. Special measures

The enemy will resort to chicanery of all sorts to suppress the church, such as the withdrawal of coal allotments or reduction of power supply. He will discontinue religious instructions in schools and will eliminate special religious instructions such as "chatechism lessons," "confirmation lessons," etc. Possibly he will replace it for instance by a state "youth initiation" or similar action.

The enemy will suppress Catholic schools and institutions; dissolve religious associations; remove Christian symbols (crosses, pictures, etc.) in public (for instance, schools, hospitals, etc.); prohibit religious magazines and books; limit and finally prohibit church services. Parents will be pressured to quit sending their children to church or religious instruction. After a while, such instruction will also be discontinued under the pretext that it is no longer necessary since it is attended only by a backward minority or not at all.

Similar procedure will be used to reduce church attendance. Church goers may be threatened with being black listed. They may be considered unsuitable for certain offices and positions for being a "backward church goer."

In many cases a so-called "public peace" is negotiated with the church after the initial wave of persecution. This is especially the case when subordinate elements have exposed themselves too much by their anti-church attitudes and have caused great attention. The subsequent period of calm is to smooth over the waves of indignation and pacify the aroused public. The church itself will, based on experience, strictly adhere to the agreements made so as not to bring on new persecutions. Through this action its hands are often tied for long periods of time.

C. Attitudes of Church in the Fight against Church

The fight against the church also has its positive aspects. It separates the former followers from the truly faithful. When the church makes sacrifices it will gain a closer relationship to those portions of the population which, until now, have remained aloof from its efforts and aims. When the church is being persecuted it will be able to do real missionary work. Greatest difficulties and highest chances of success are thus directly related.

The church must concentrate upon fighting against intolerance and a personality cult.

The church must emphasize the fact that each of God's commandments will be revenged sooner or later.

It must cultivate the concept of "help thy neighbor" and designate as such all persecuted persons.

It must call attention to the responsibilities of a Christian, such as resisting the misuse of power, disobeying edicts impinging on freedom to worship; and must remind the people that children not only belong to their parents but should be brought up by them.

5. Propagation of Dissension Among the Population in Occupied Areas.

In order to consolidate his power, the enemy will attempt to set one group or class against another.

Examples:

City dwellers →	Foster distrust toward the country folk. Instigate dissension between consumers and producers. Discredit the farm population.
Farmers →	Foster distrust toward city dwellers. Foster distrust toward the working class. Aggravate resentment toward large land owners. Instigate dissension between producers and consumers.
Working class →	Create antagonism toward farmers. Aggravate resentment against the middle class. Foster distrust against intellectuals and the church.
Middle class →	Foster distrust of the working class.
Artisans →	Cultivate resentment toward working class. Stir up distrust against commerce and industry.

To divide and conquer is the enemy's favorite tactic.

By temporary concessions to one or the other section of the population or group, he will attempt to obtain their approval and loyal cooperation.

Do not fall for this well planned scheme to increase internal dissension. The tune will soon change. The enemy will only favor you as long as he needs you. Once he has accomplished his goal, he will drop you without any qualms. A complete 180° reversal in his course of operations will not bother him. He has been used to such radical changes for decades.

If you agree to join the game and are short-sighted enough to pursue small group and special interests against your fellow citizens, you will only aid the enemy and exhaust yourself. Nothing could be of greater advantage to him.

6. Tactics Usd by Enemy in Destroying Clubs and Associations

Clubs and associations disliked by the enemy will not be prohibited at once, but will be initially subjected to various types of harassment, etc.

If he immediately prohibits such organizations, he takes the risk of having membership lists destroyed. Therefore, he will only be able to apprehend leaders and prominent officials whereas the mass of the members will be able to go underground. A reorganization of the smashed organization, taking place later and illegally, is thus facilitated since the enemy does not have the membership lists.

He will thus proceed carefully by observing and registering for the time being. He will also avoid smashing local branches of organizations prematurely so as not to alarm the others.

When the enemy has obtained the membership lists he will destroy and outlaw the organizations. The State Security Service will watch former members in order to stifle any attempt to reorganize the club or association.

The enemy will never oppose all clubs at the same time. His power would be insufficient to do so. He will rather suppress them individually, and at different times. He will suppress organizations in the following sequence.

1. Political parties —Social Democratic Party
   —Middle Class Parties

2. Unions

3. Youth Organizations	—Political —Church —Political and non-denominational
4. Church	—Catholic church —Reformed church —Independent religious groups

7. Enemy Liquidation of Certain Classes of the Population.

The enemy will eliminate certain classes or section of the population that he dislikes. During these "special operations" he will gradually increase the severity of class repression.

Normally this will take place as follows:

First, he will dismiss only those in key positions.

then ↓

He will prohibit them from working in certain professions. He will force these classes to make contributions.

then ↓

The enemy will bar these individuals from all types of work. He will then withdraw food ration cards since these individuals are "non-workers."

They will be discriminated against by being prohibited from entering certain places. They may be forced to wear identifying insignia.

They will be prohibited from owning vehicles, radios, or telephones, and prohibited from purchasing books and magazines.

then ↓

They will be deported to forced labor camps and liquidated.

III. Operations of the Resistance Movement

1. Procedure of the Resistance Movement

Phase 1: Period of Observation and Evaluation.

Be patient, allow the population to recuperate. Time will work for you.

Observe the enemy and study his peculiarities.

Sort out the population as follows:

a. Who can be considered for active collaboration?
b. Who hesitates?
c. Who acts passively or is indifferent?
d. Who has joined the enemy's ranks?

Phase 2: Organization of passive resistance.

Form cells by bringing together several persons who know and respect each other well.

Establish connection with other cells.

Consolidate the various cells. As soon as they become too large (more than ten persons) divide them and form new ones.

Group several cells under a leader. They will then form a circle. As soon as several such circles exist, and the underground organization has reached a certain degree of development, you will begin forming special sections.

Phase 3—Commencement of resistance operations.

Inform the population about appropriate behavior toward the enemy.

Remove persecuted persons from the reach of the police by, warning, hiding, or assisting them escape. Organize a propaganda machine. Isolate agents and informers. Initiate acts of sabotage.

Keep traitors and informers in check by counter terror. Make it as dangerous to work for the enemy as it is to work against him.

Continue to maintain passive and active resistance, until the occupation power has been weakened by events beyond our command and guerrilla operations to the extent that open insurrection can be initiated.

2. Concealment of Weapons and Ammunition from the Enemy

In practically every Swiss household you will find weapons and ammunition.

They must be removed from the reach of the enemy when the country is occupied.

To supplement arms on hand, also collect small arms and ammunition which, during the fighting, have been left in your area either by our own or by enemy troops.

Keep these weapons until guerrilla detachments or the resistance movement need them. Weapons must be cleverly concealed as their illegal possession may mean a death sentence.

The best method of concealing munitions is by burying them. In order to protect the weapons from considerable damage due to humidity, proceed as follows:

Insure that the weapon is completely dry before covering them with a heavy layer of grease (only use weapons grease).

Close off the muzzle by means of a stopper made of grease or wax.

Wrap a rag soaked in oil around the bolt.

Wrap the entire weapon in a large cloth. Tie the cloth with strings.

Place the weapon into a wooden box.

Cover the joints of the box with wax (such as candle wax).

Put a piece of tar paper around the box.

Bury the box at a dry place, if possible in a building (such as a cellar with gravel ground, barn with natural ground, sheltered places, etc.).

Check, clean and grease the weapon about once every two to three months.

Pack ammunition as follows: (loose rounds, packages, cases, individual hand grenades).

Wrap the individual packages of ammunition in about ten layers of newspapers. Place the packages into a wooden box whose bottom is covered with about 5 centimeters of dry sawdust. Close and wrap the box similar to the weapons container.

The sawdust will absorb any humidity that may enter the box. Ammunition is very sensitive to humidity; as a result, you must change newspaper and sawdust about once every two months and air the ammunition for a while.

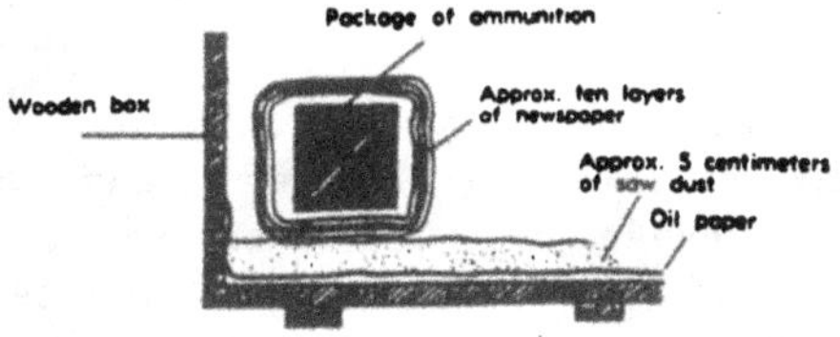

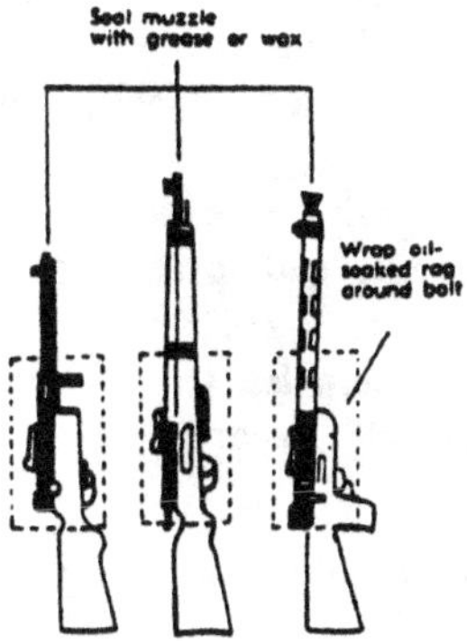

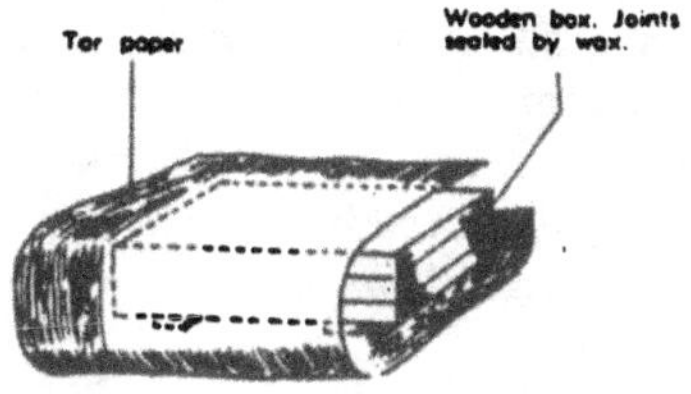

WEAPONS BOX

3. Concealment of Radios from the Enemy

Hide your radio immediately since the enemy will soon confiscate all radio sets in order to interrupt the last connection through the "Iron Curtain" of the occupation.

He will want to lower your morale by preventing information from the free world or from your government in exile from reaching you.

4. Manufacture of Illegal Printed Matter

A. Manufacture by individuals

In the manufacture of underground newspapers, leaflets, etc., you must distinguish between items produced by individuals and items produced in a print shop.

Individuals can produce several hundred copies of leaflets by typewriter, or various types of stamps.

Equipment used to produce such material is inconspicuous and can be easily hidden.

There are several advantages to this type of operation. The raw material—paper and ink—are easy to obtain. There is no noise during the printing.

By working alone, you are relatively secure.

Circulation will be small but this disadvantage is compensated for by the utilization of many individuals.

Arrest of single individuals will not compromise the entire operation.

B. Small shop

A small shop utilizing mimeograph and stencil machines can print several thousand copies of leaflets, etc. The machinery is relatively small and can be hidden easily. It is easy to procure raw material—paper, stencils, colors. Such machines make little noise when operated. Such machines can be found in large numbers everywhere and can often be utilized when not being used for their normal work.

If, during a search of private homes, supplies or paper and reproduction machines are found, the inhabitants will face imprisonment or execution. If possible, use machines which are serving legal means known to everybody, for your secret enterprise. Conceal your paper supply inconspicuously with other "legal" paper supplies.

C. Large operation

With printing presses found in shops or publishing firms you can reproduce ten to 100,000 copies of the items you wish to distribute.

Advantages and disadvantages:

A large circulation can be effected in a short period of time. Each type of publication. from the handbill to the poster, is possible. However, security problems increase as several people must be brought into the operation in order to operate the presses; the machines create considerable noise during operation. The quantity of paper, type and ink will be correspondingly larger and may be difficult to obtain.

D. The following security measures should be observed:

Burn the carbon paper used, do not simply throw it away; waste papers (bad copies) must be burned as are stencils, rough-drafts, and manuscripts that are no longer needed. Each time material is burned, stir ashes with a stick as the enemy can read the charred pages with the technical aides he has at his disposal.

Also, melt type and disassemble hand compositions. Camouflage noise of a large press by running the engine of a vehicle in front of the building; operating an air hammer nearby; turning on several radios full blast.

E. Design of Illegal Printed Matter:

Several people will be involved in designing posters, writing script for radio broadcasts and articles for underground newspapers.

Staff

Military collaborator Political collaborator Jointly explain war events	Artist for Cartoons Drawings and captions	Humorist Satirist Create jokes about the new regime

If you are using a well-known, talented personality whose style of drawing or verse is well known, he can only collaborate if he goes "underground." Under certain circumstances, this individual may only supply ideas and rough copies; an unknown person will then do the master copy. Anybody who can be recognized by virtue of his style, will be immediately arrested.

The ban against listening to foreign radio stations or the confiscation of radio sets as well as censorship of the press, will increase the need for objective news and in turn the need for and importance of leaflets and underground newspapers.

5. Propaganda

A. Distribution of leaflets

Do not distribute leaflets to strangers on the street since an informer may be among them. Throw leaflets into mail boxes in stairwells. This can be best done by people wearing postal uniforms. He who receives a leaflet should not keep it but will pass it on to reliable acquaintances. The radius of contact will thus be increased and the most modest means of the underground movement will have the greatest possible effect.

B. Distribution of Underground Newspapers

Distribute underground newspaper to persons whom you know well. They in turn will pass them on to acquaintances who will read them and pass them on. Insert a request at the end of each newspaper and leaflet that the contents be copied by typewriter and circulated.

C. Section for painting slogans on walls—writing slogans on walls.

Slogans written on walls are a good means to keep the masses aroused. Slogans must be as simple as possible. It is best to use catch phrases; single letters or symbolic signs such as the "V" for victory were used by the western resistance movements during World War II.

Slogans are best smeared on sidewalks and walls with oil paint and large brushes. If necesary, chalk, held sideways so that a wide stroke can be effected, may be used. However, chalk is easily washed off. Oil paint, on the other hand, sticks to the object and can be made illegible only by repainting.

Large numbers of slogans, appearing night after night, will make the enemy nervous and raise the self-confidence of the population since such activities demonstrate the inefficiency of the occupation forces and the power of the resistance movement.

D. Destruction of enemy posters

Official notifications or announcements of the occupation forces, as well as propaganda posters supporting the enemy ideology, must be opposed or you will slowly "drown" in the flood of propaganda.

Special sections should be created to tear off, scrape off, paint over these posters or paste over them with resistance posters.

If the enemy surveillance of streets is ineffectual, use the cheap but time-consuming method of partially scraping or pasting over these posters. However, if surveillance is effective and tight, be satisfied with pasting across the official poster a relatively small ribbon of paper bearing the inscription "Nothing but lies." This will require little time and does not create any noise.

Equipment used by sections: paint bucket, spatulas to scrape off enemy posters, rubber soled or tennis shoes, (noiseless) and perhaps bicycles as they are fast and make no noise.

Keep in mind that a typewriter is often more important than a pistol, a reproduction machine is worth as much as a light machine gun. The State Security Service fears underground newspapers and leaflets almost more than weapons and explosives.

6. Conditioning of Resistance Leaders or Members Engaged in Extremely Hazardous Tasks.

Just like your comrades in the guerrilla detachments who prepare their operations down to the smallest detail and train on certain phases at their camp prior to the commencement of the operation, you are required to train your most important members in behavior during house search by the State Security Service and behavior during interrogation.

A. Training on behavior during house search.

As instructors, utilize former police officials who know the techniques of house search and members of the resistance movement who have experienced house searches by the State Security Service and are acquainted with its methods.

These house searches, conducted as part of the training, must be carried out in the same manner as those of the State Security Service in order to obtain as much realism as possible.

The purpose of such drill is to show your comrade mistakes he made in his behavior; to strengthen his nerves by conditioning him to nerve-wrecking situations; and to demonstrate mistakes made in hiding contraband.

B. Training for behavior during interrogations.

Here again, use as instructors former police or law officials who are versed in the technique of interrogation. People who have previously been interrogated by the State Security Service may be able to give valuable tips, and last but not least, be a living example that "one can survive such interrogations."

7. "Going Underground". Selection and Use of Hide-outs

Chiefs and important members of the resistance movement must maintain several safehouses in the same city or district in order to hold conferences, or to go underground temporarily or permanently, if necessary. Likely places for such hide-outs are seldom used apartments, warehouses, homes of friends, or vacation cottages. Sometimes it may be necessary to commute continually on railroads or subways for a period of time.

8. Security of Safe Areas.

Locations which you must visit frequently, such as hide-outs, homes of friends, etc., must be made secure by using simple signs. Design a system of signals to indicate whether a location is secure by predesignated placement of shutters, flower pots; arrangement of curtains; open or closed windows; or clothes hanging on clothes lines.

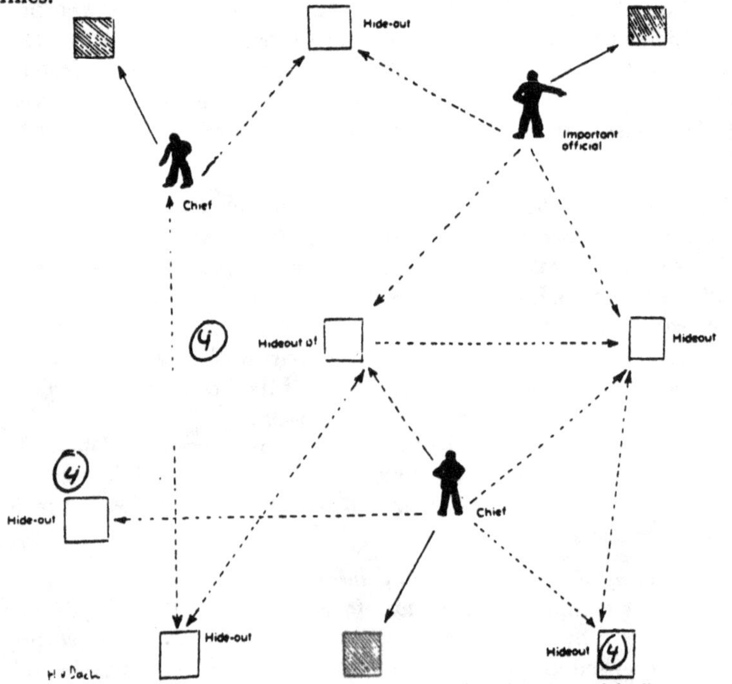

No written material will be kept in a hide-out

Hide-outs are known only to a small group of selected persons.

No one knows all hide-outs. Especially important resistance leaders must have an individual hide-out which is unknown to anyone, even his family.

Store food and water at the hide-outs so that you can hide for several days without exposing yourself.

These signs must be able to be recognized from some distance so that in case of danger you have the possibility of passing inconspicuously by the house.

This rudimentary security system may be compromised if, for instance, the inhabitants are arrested unexpectedly by the State Security Service before they have time to post the normal warning sign. For this reason, an additional security refinement must be developed and be of such a nature that you can activate it even when you are being led off in handcuffs.

For example, place a flower stand in the stairwell and "accidentally" knock it over when you are being dragged by, etc.

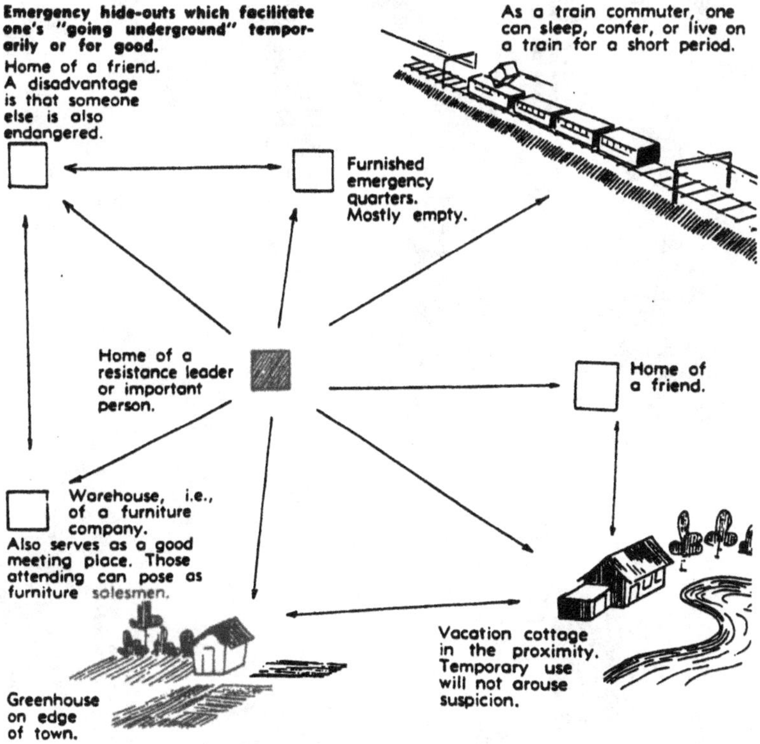

9. Security of Underground Conferences

A. Selection of meeting place:

Meetings of resistance members must be prepared at least as carefully as a raid, for they constitute a "special type" of operation.

Security of an underground meeting.

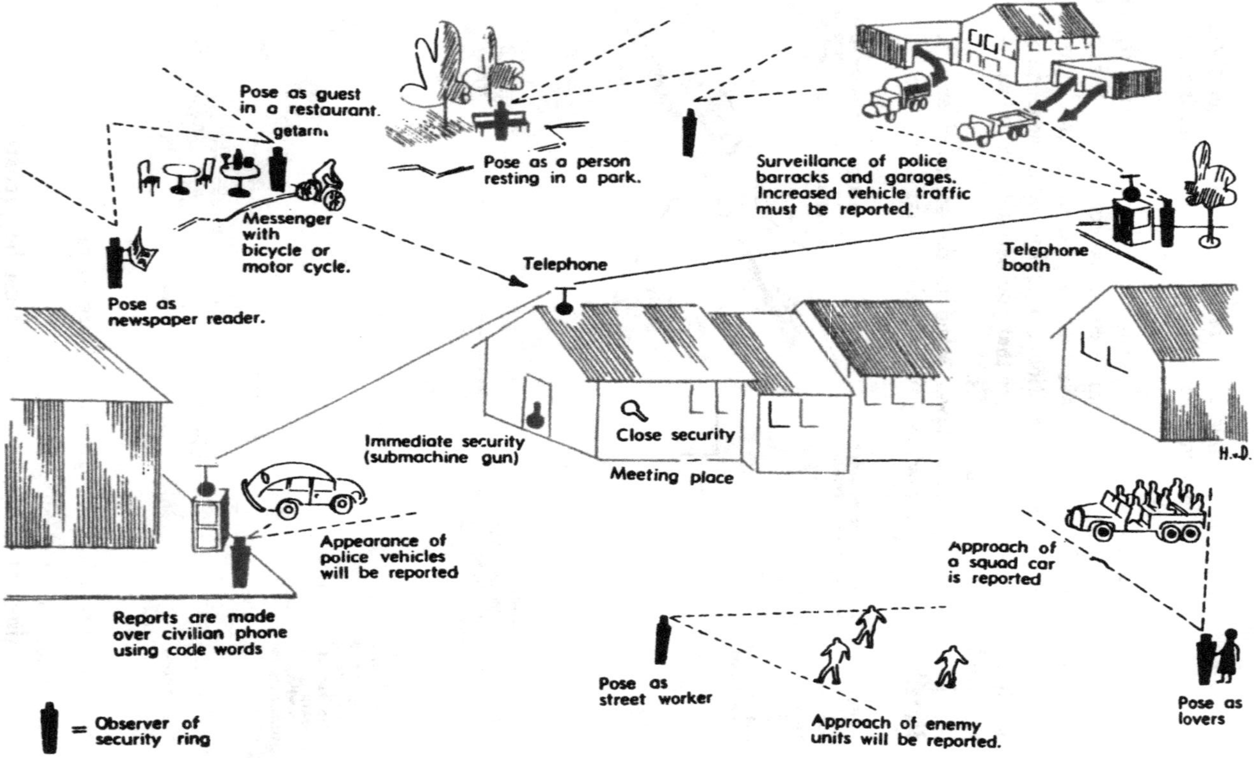

A suitable place, for instance, might be in amongst row houses as searching and encirclement are made very difficult and time-consuming for the enemy. Consequently, you may gain sufficient time to escape.

Individual buildings in the open can be easily surrounded and then raided. Avoid them.

B. Behavior of participant going and returning:

From the moment you leave your home you must consider yourself in "combat with the State Security Service" and be more careful than a soldier on reconnaissance patrol. Your type of fight is more ennervating, takes longer and is more cruel than any fight on the front of a "conventional war."

Observe the street prior to leaving home to see if your house is being watched. Be as inconspicuous as possible once on the street. Watch out for repeated appearances of the same person who might be an informer, or member of the State Security Service shadowing you. Faces are hard to remember; thus pay attention to clothing.

When checking to determine if you are being followed, do not turn around in a conspicuous manner. Instead, casually glance to the rear while crossing the street, lighting a cigarette, unfolding a newspaper, entering or leaving a shop.

Use the public transportation system (streetcar), but during rush hours; the fuller they are the less likely anyone will be able to follow you.

C. Security for meeting place:

Distinguish between outer "security ring" and "inner security" ring. The outer security ring consisting of observers will be some distance from the meeting place. The inner security ring will be in the meeting place itself.

Members of the outer security ring will observe routes of access and warn of the approach of police either on foot or in vehicles. Police buildings and garages should be watched to ascertain if more vehicles than usual are leaving. Warnings will be passed on by civilian telephone using code words.

Inner security of the meeting will consist of one guard on the ground floor with a pistol or submachine gun and one observer on one of the upper floors who will move from window to window.

D. Preparations in case of enemy action:

Before the meeting convenes you must determine if you are going to fight or run if discovered by the enemy. If you choose to fight, designate who is to serve as rear guard and who is to escape and what material must be removed. Designate predetermined escape routes.

If you choose to bluff your way through, develop a good cover story; determine who is to hide what and how.

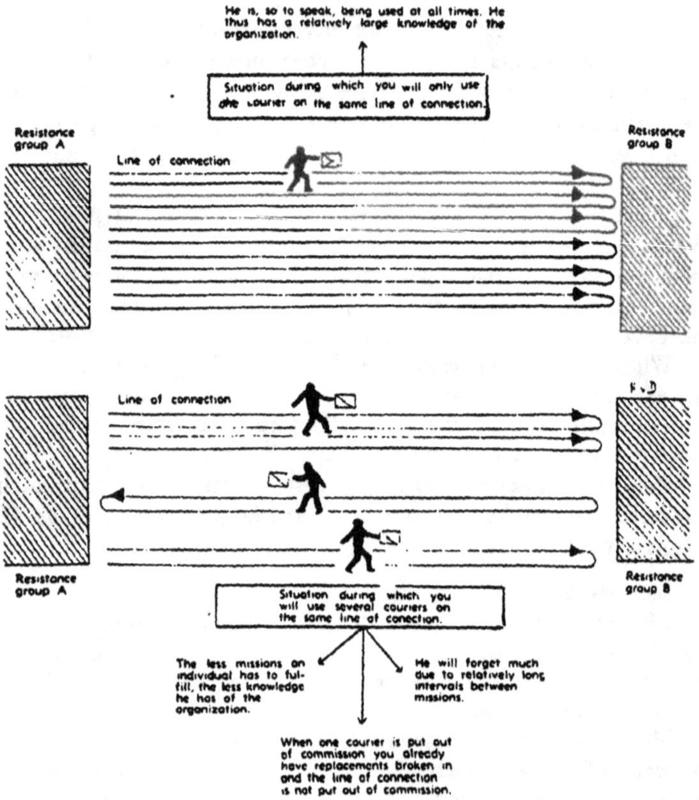

10. Courier Service

It is imperative to develop a communications net in order to transmit orders and directives quickly as well as warnings of impending police action.

As means of communication you will use: couriers; the public telephone system; civilian postal system, and clandestine transmitters.

You must distinguish between:

"Tactical couriers" used for the internal communication in a small area, and

"Operational couriers" used for cross-country communication. They also may be used to maintain contact with the government in exile.

Suitable couriers are:

a. In rural areas: Door-to-door salesmen Cattle dealers Veterinarians	Persons who travel a lot without causing suspicion	"Tactical Couriers" (Close Communication)
b. In urban areas: Collectors for gas and electric companies Mailmen, errand boys, truckers	Persons who can move about easily without causing suspicion	
c. Cross-country RR personnel RR-postal employees Personnel of airlines	Often can move about for long distances without arousing suspicion	"Operational Couriers" (Cross-country communication)

The Courier service

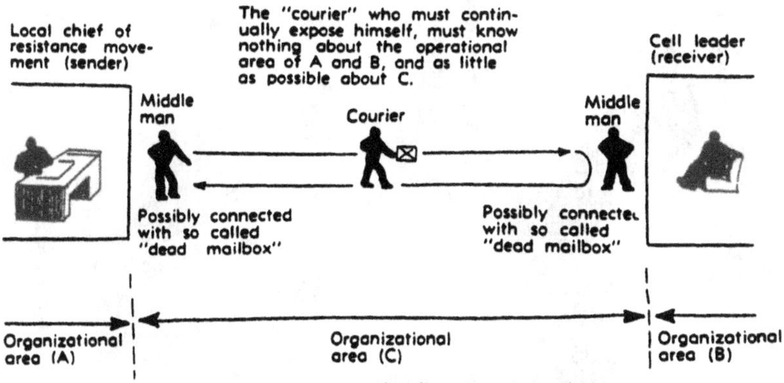

Your couriers are continually exposed to the danger of being apprehended. As a rule, they should thus know neither the sender nor the receiver, for these are the chiefs of the organization. For security measures, insert "middlemen" who accept messages or deliver them for transmittal.

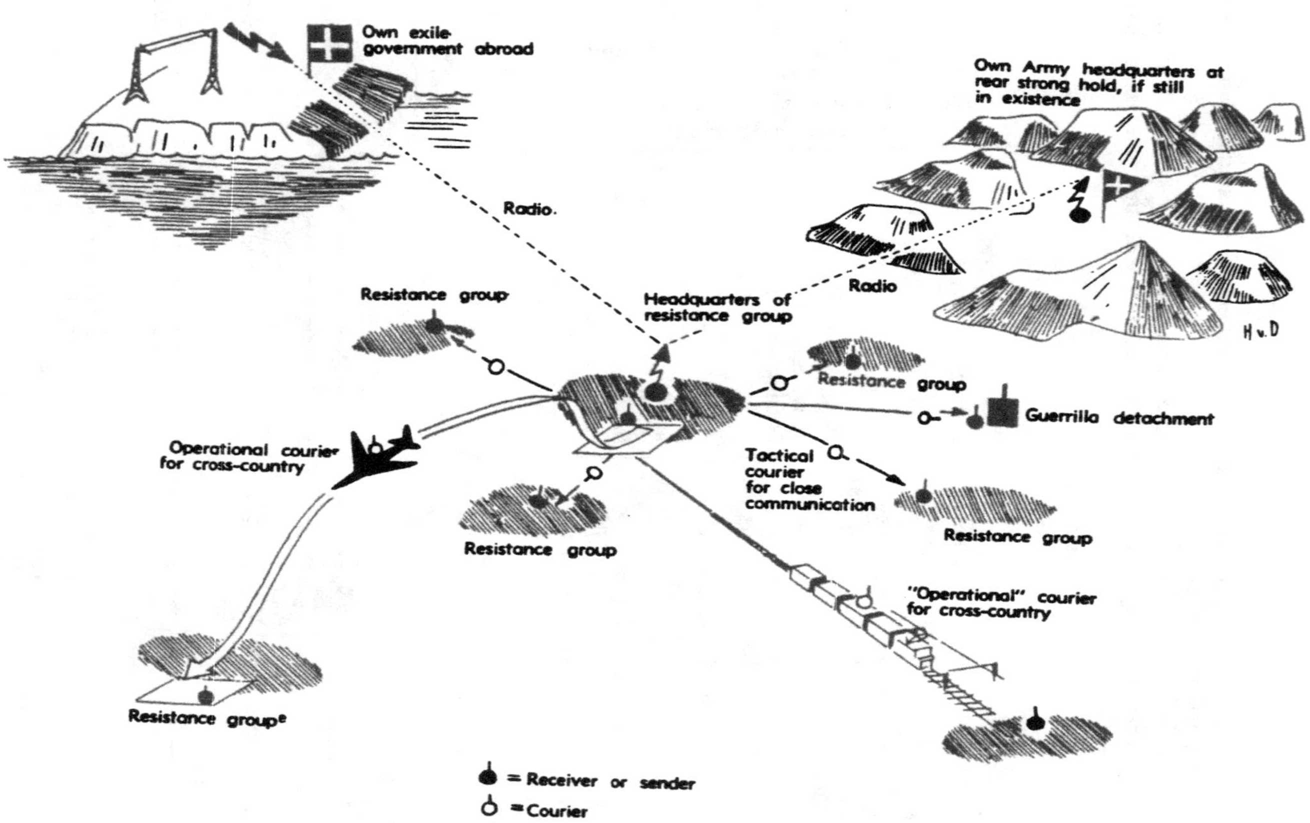
Own exile government abroad
Own Army headquarters at rear strong hold, if still in existence
Radio.
Radio
Headquarters of resistance group
Resistance group
Resistance group
Guerrilla detachment
Tactical courier for close communication
Resistance group
Resistance group
Operational courier for cross-country
Resistance group
"Operational" courier for cross-country
H v. D
= Receiver or sender
= Courier

Security of a resistance radio station during operation.

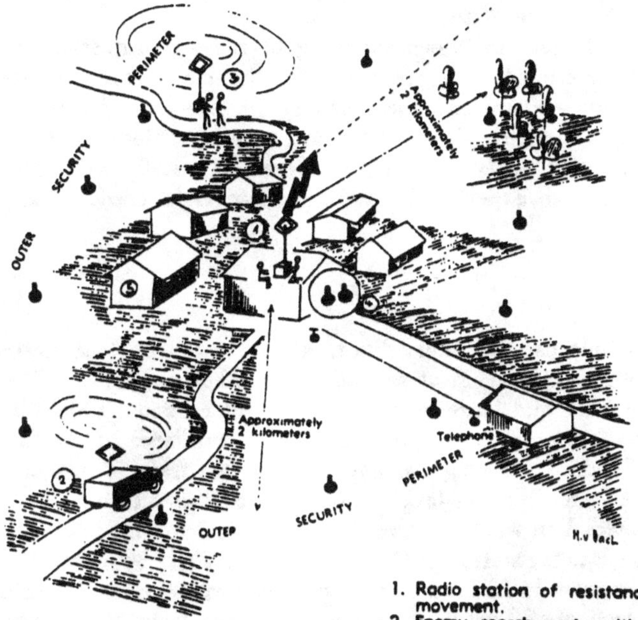

Inner security ring of radio station

Security guard in civilian clothes, poses as harmless country laborer, logger, street cleaner, etc.

Guards are to report the presence of enemy search elements with direction finder apparatus so that the underground station may stop sending messages in time. Reporting means: civilian telephone (code), bicycle, motorcycle.

1. Radio station of resistance movement.
2. Enemy search party with direction finder apparatus on vehicle attempting to locate clandestine sender.
3. Search party with direction finder apparatus on foot.
4. Inner security ring of radio station.
5. Prepared hide-out about 500 meters from sender in order to be able to "disappear" when search begins.

Transmittal of messages by radio

Only use radios. The only extensive use of radios should be in contacting higher headquarters of the resistance movement and our government in exile in allied countries or our own Army headquarters (remainder of Army at rear stronghold) if the latter still exists.

It is worthwhile to expend a great deal of effort in establishing radio security measures. Messages should be sent in code. The radio station should be camouflaged and guarded. During tactical situations, within the resistance movement, do not use radios. For here you have to transmit many messages daily. As a result, radio security is made difficult and the effort expended for security is too great in relation to the value of the various messages.

Do not forget that the monitoring of radio transmissions and the use of direction finders are easier for the enemy than the interception of couriers who disappear among the hundreds of thousands of citizens. In order to place your radio communications under surveillance, he only needs a handful of clever, technically well trained and well equipped experts. To intercept couriers he needs an army of policemen.

11. Use of Trains

If possible use secondary lines. Always travel on local trains. Board and leave the train at secondary or suburban stations. Main railroad stations and large trains (express, international trains) are more likely to be subject to more thorough surveillance by the State Security Service. Checking passengers while the train is in motion is more likely to occur in large trains than on "slow trains."

Example: You want to travel from Bern to Luzern. Walk or use the bus to get to the station at Ostermundingen. There board the local train to Langnau. In Langnau transfer to the next "slow train" going in the direction of Luzern. However, leave the train at the small station in Littau, four kilometers before reaching Luzern, and then walk the rest of the way.

12. Neutralizing Informers

A. Aims of enemy

By using informers, the enemy hopes to collect information on your activities; sow distrust; make contact among members of the resistance more difficult.

Nobody can trust his neighbor anymore. As a result, the organization of the resistance movement, especially in its initial stage, becomes very difficult.

Techniques of using informers can be seen in the following diagram:

Informer Headquarters of the State Security Service

Informer Reserve

"Movable reserve," so to speak

Used only occasionally, for instance during demonstrations, strikes, unrests, revolts.

The "informer reserve" is composed of the most skilled and qualified individuals.

Permanent Net of Informers

"local forces" are used permanently in each

- Block
- Shop
- Factory
- School, etc.

From this group is used the "mass," or the average informer

Operational Area of Informers
1. Clearing of personal questions

Momentary Problems

Surveillance of *momentarily* interesting persons

- Suspects to be shadowed and against whom material is to be collected
- Persons looked upon unfavorably and who are to be used later (recruited) for own aims

Permanent Problems

Surveillance of *permanently* interesting persons

Enemies, Potential enemies such as:

- Former politicians
- Union officials
- Editors
- Former officers
- Former police
- Officials
- Teachers
- Priests

"Friends" Evaluation of political reliability ("faithful to party line") of personalities from among own ranks, for instance:

- Key administration officials
- Party officials
- Police officials
- Organs of occupation troops

Operational Area of Informers
2. Clearing up Questions of Opinion and Technical Problems

Specifics

What is the "opinion":
- of their own police
- of their own occupation troops
- of their own administration
- in the factories (working class)
  - work enthusiasm (production)
  - Sabotage/passive resistance suppy of population

General

What is the public opinion of the population (masses):
- what is the attitude toward the "system"
- what are the reactions to the various measures taken by the occupation forces (dismantling, terror, etc.)

B. Recruiting Informers

The State Security Service will thoroughly investigate the past and present of those people who seem to be likely prospects as informers. Above all it is essential to collect material with which he may be able to blackmail the victims at the appropriate moment. In this respect not only political opinion but also one's private life are of interest.

The following are points which are of special interest to the State Security Service:

Does he have debts?

Does he have other financial difficulties?

Does everything work well in his marriage or is there a possibility of black mail?

Does he have a girl friend?

Did he commit a foolish act sometime in the past which is carefully hidden from his present associates?

Is he extraordinarily ambitious?

Is he bitter, dissatisfied and on bad terms with society?

Finally, the following are recruited as informers:

1. Politically incriminated persons who are given the choice of either working for the State Security Service or being liquidated.

2. Families of political opponents under arrest and imprisoned or in concentration camps. In this case both threats and temptation are used by promising execution or torture in case of refusal or easing conditions of imprisonment or even release in case of cooperation.

Blackmail (about 20%)

3. People indulging in tax evasion, the black market, etc.

4. Criminals who are promised release from prison or no sentence.

5. Sexually abnormal persons

6. Alcoholics

7. Drug addicts

More or less volunteers (about 60%)

8. Those lacking character who are willing to do anything for money.

9. Idealists who have fallen for the "system" and are so blind ideologically that they are willing to perform even the dirtiest jobs.

Volunteers (about 20%)

C. *Defense Against Informers*

Passive measures used against informers:

Discuss confidential subjects only in closed rooms never in a streetcar, railroad or restaurant. Speak only with persons whom you trust and whom you have known for years.

When a third party arrives change the subject in an inconspicuous manner.

By maintaining a persistent silence in public the best source of information for informers will dry up. It is easier for them to pick up pieces of conversation in public than to infiltrate a group of people known to each other; in this group a personal atmosphere exists where an individual's thinking and past are known to one another.

Active measures to defend against informers:

The meeting place for an informer is never located in the headquarters of the State Security Service but always in some plain restaurant where informers can come and go without being recognized or drawing attention. Insurance agencies, travel bureaus, etc., are very suitable as meeting places since in the constant stream of people, informers will not draw undue attention to themselves.

Locate and observe these meeting places.

Attempt to identify informers and thereby neutralize them.

Insure that their identity is made known to the population through the use of wall posters, handbills and rumors.

13. How to Meet the Danger of Being Overheard.

Modern construction methods with its minimal wall thicknesses generally increases the chances of listening in. Prior to a conversation, close doors and windows.

Do not speak in those rooms of your home which adjoin a neighboring apartment or the stairwell. You thus prevent involuntary "overhearing" of your conversation but also a deliberate "listening" by your neighbor.

If you have roomers or if you possess only one room turn on the radio. Its noise will drown out your conversation and prevents being overheard.

If you fear that your home is bugged by the State Security Service, turn on the radio prior to secret discussions. Select a station approved by the enemy and turn it up to full volume. Any microphones will thus only pick up the noise of the radio.

Apart from that, do not fear the danger of bugging too much. Microphones are seldom used for obvious reasons.

14. Behavior During Interrogation

If several officials of the State Security Service knock you down in the interrogation cellar, do not remain in their midst. This way they can all hit you at the same time. Attempt to reach a corner of the room. Thus only two or three men can strike you at the same time. The rest would only hinder each other.

Do not attempt to remain upright as long as possible. Play the role of the "dead" or "seriously injured." Fall down on the floor and roll over onto your stomach. Your sensitive organs are thus in the center of a protective rib or bone cage. Kicking and clubbing will cause less damage. In addition pull in your chin and attempt to protect your kidneys by pressing your elbows against your body.

Always answer in a vague and indeterminate manner. The basic rule to follow during an interrogation is: "To say as little as possible." Keep in mind that the police cannot read your thoughts. They will blind you with glaring lights while the interrogation officials sit in the dark.

Deny and refute everything, even when the accusations can be proved. At least you will make propaganda this way.

Avoid mentioning names. Since you are considered a "state enemy," everyone whom you know will also be suspected a potential enemy.

Hollering, threats and mistreatment are among the methods used by the State Security Service. You must realize this.

Do not be deceived by "friendship" of the State Security Service. This is only a technique used to throw you off your guard. The interrogating officials will show their true face soon enough.

You can expect the following: solitary confinement; confinement in dark cell; and confinement in "small cells," called "upright coffins," which prevent you from sitting or lying down.

You will be prevented from going to sleep by guards who will arouse you each time you begin to fall asleep.

You can expect general mistreatment, such as beatings, removal of teeth, extraction of finger and toe nails, being dabbed with a lighted cigarette, etc.

They will attempt to demoralize you with horrible news, hunger, cold or thirst.

15. Behavior in Forced Labor Camp (Concentration Camp)

A. Organization

By order of the camp administration, a "barracks senior" often has to be selected for each barracks; sometimes a "camp senior" has to be designated also. Where this is not the case you must do this on your own since by building an organization among the prisoners you can improve the living conditions considerably.

The net thus installed by the camp administration for technical reasons (contact with inmates) has to be used by you for your own purposes and even secretly improved.

You must distinguish between:

Camp net (comprises the entire camp) and

Barracks net (comprises the various barracks)

In camps with less control you are able to build both nets, whereas in camps run with strict discipline you can only institute the barracks net.

In the barracks net the chief is the "barracks senior." His aids are the confidants of the barracks inmates.

In the camp net the chief is the "camp senior." His aids are the barracks seniors.

The barracks or camp seniors are responsible for contact between the masses of inmates and the camp administration (accept orders; submit requests; i.e., obtain permission to write letters, receive mail, visits, permission to smoke, etc.; submission of protests and complaints pertaining to treatment, food supply, billets, heating, hygiene, etc.)

Assign as many missions as possible in the secretly organized net. By virtue of the fact that one has an office (mission) and must help others, his own problems will recede into the background. The more people assigned a mission in a barracks, the greater the possibility of maintaining the will to resist for long periods.

B. General

Take care of new arrivals. They are naturally more demoralized. Instruct new arrivals about the general camp conditions and appropriate behavior by a specially selected individual. If they are left alone their will to resist threatens to collapse. Then the enemy has reached his goal. As old inmates you have to take preventive measures.

You can maintain the will to resist and morale by a variety of methods:

Build the above mentioned organizations among inmates, in order to strengthen the feeling of solidarity and to improve living conditions.

Spread true news about the world situation so as to foster the belief in the victory of the good cause. Organize singing and discussion groups.

Establish "package groups" in which each member will put his package at the disposition of the group. Even the most lonely persons will thus share in tobacco products and additional food items and perhaps items of clothing.

Trusted individuals will inform the inmates about the general political and military situation (some information will always filter through); issue instructions on behavior for the immediate future; issue directives on what will be discussed the following day with the guards during work (political conversion).

Together with the political inmates a certain number of common criminals will be imprisoned at the same time; they are to disturb the solidarity of the camp. You have to spot them soon and subdue them. They are very often informers.

C. Details concerning camp or barracks net

Organization of medical care:

In many cases, the sick or injured are not admitted to the sick bay or are returned to work too soon because of maliciousness or lack of space. Without care given by comrades, the will to live to instinct for self-preservation will be quickly snuffed out and they quickly die.

Organize a barracks aid service. You will, of course, lack medicine, first aid material and instruments. But this is not so important. The whole thing is rather a psychological problem. If the sick or injured feels that his society is taking care of him, he will muster inner strength.

Possible ways of helping the sick when lacking first aid material include:

In summertime, give him the coolest place; in wintertime the warmest spot in the barracks.

Quench his thirst; if possible, give him additional food items which the strongest have saved.

Give him something to smoke.

Cool him off with wet cloths or give him additional blankets obtained from those in better physical condition.

Assign him the lightest duties if sick individuals have to work.

Take care of him generally.

In each barracks system is a former doctor, pharmacist, student of medicine, first aid man, or some other suitable individual who can assume the role of a "nurse."

Organization of Ministry:

Each will reach a point of low morale when the last hope for life seems to disappear completely and a person is no longer able to believe in the future. To cope with this problem, the prison community has to step in through the organization of a ministry service. For this purpose use doctors. priests, lay priests, salvation army members, etc.

You will not lack qualified personnel outlined above for they are always subjected to special hate campaigns by the regime and are the first ones to be thrown into prison.

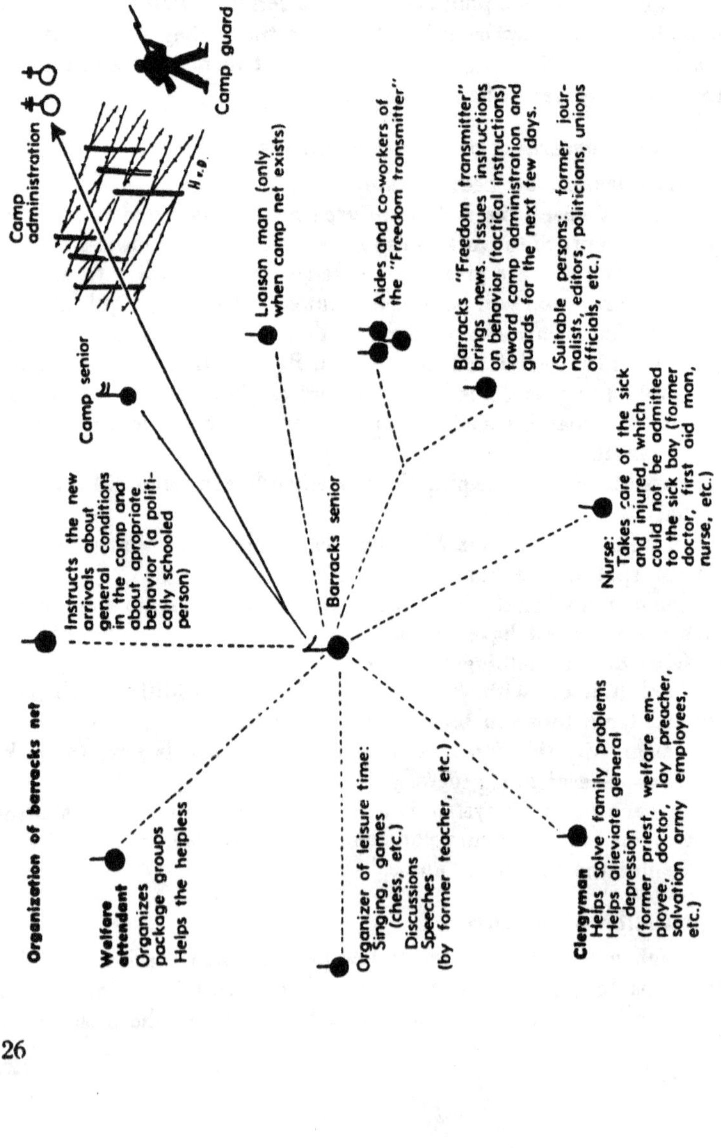

D. Relationship to camp guards

Guards will always consist of two types, sadists and the decent ones who only go along with everything because they are forced to do so but condemn any excessive acts; yet they must remain silent. You must take advantage of this situation.

Tactics: Drive a moral wedge in between the two types of the camp guards. Method: Find out who is decent. Talk with the guards (primarily during work).

It is hammered into the guards that the inmates are the scum of humanity. By exemplary fellowship you must demonstrate and prove to the guards that you are very decent people. Once this has succeeded you have won the first round and, at the same time, you will have pricked the belief of the guards in the infallibility of the regime.

Never talk to a group of guards. Groups are always more agressive and meaner than individuals. In a group, the individual is first a "member of an organization" and then only a "human being." As an individual, however, he is primarily a "human being" and secondarily a "member of the organization." As a result, always approach individuals.

E. Passive resistance

Passive resistance and actions of protests are, of course, very difficult to implement. Nevertheless, even here there are several possibilities. Below is an example:

If an inmate has been killed during an interrogation, "shot while escaping" or has been officially executed, sing in the next few days "I had a comrade" often and demonstratively. The meaning of the song will even be understood by a guard speaking a foreign language.

16. Passive Resistance

General behavior

There are many types of passive resistance that can be utilized by housewives, children and the unemployed.

If members of the occupation troops or collaborators enter a streetcar, a bus or a restaurant, discontinue all, even the most harmless, conversation and let cold silence take over. If you are talked to directly, answer coolly and as curtly as possible. Also pretend you have a date or urgent business to take care of in order to cut short the conversation and leave.

Never return the greetings of the enemy but disregard him on purpose. When he wants to hold open the door or wants to help you get in or out of a vehicle, do not accept.

Do not take a place in the same train compartment as the enemy, but rather stand in the aisle. If necessary, change cars.

If only a few pedestrians are on the street, leave the sidewalk and go to the opposite side when a member of the occupation forces approaches. You can even enter a stairwell of a house for a minute. This technique is, of course, only practical when not too many people are on the street and your behavior will be noticed.

If the enemy is waiting at a train station, streetcar station, in front of a movie or at the theater, step back so that a large circle will form in midst of the waiting crowd; this will make him realize the moral isolation to which he is subjected.

Women and daughters: When you are asked to dance by members of the occupation forces or by their collaborators, refuse under pretext of being tired, having no desire to dance, or being ill.

In all those places where you have collective electric meters—not your private meter—burn as many lamps as possible at all times (for instance, stairwell, and cellars). By your increasing the power consumption a shortage will occur thus causing bottlenecks in industry and transportation. Since you cannot let the lights burn at night because of the strict black-out without causing attraction, do this during daytime. This has the additional advantage that it will coincide with the peak hours of consumption by industry which is especially effective.

Behavior during quarters requisitioning

It is very unlikely that the enemy will billet individual military personnel with the population. For obvious reasons he will keep them together where they can be easily controlled and protected.

If, however, contrary to all expectations, the enemy billets personnel with the population or you have to accept a collaborator, proceed as follows:

a. If he only has one room in your home, disturb his sleep by playing the radio as loudly as possible. If the radio has been requisitioned, have the children make an infernal racket.

Call him to the telephone at any odd hour of the night. The phone will then have been either hung up or he will have to listen to some derogatory remark. Mobilize all of your acquaintances for these calls.

b. When he has his own place, ring his bell anytime during the day or night. Push in the bell button and squeeze in a match so that it will stick in the bell and thus ring continuously. It is very unpleasant to be awakened up out of deep sleep and have to run downstairs from the fourth floor in order to remove the disturbance.

Always throw pieces of paper containing threats and reproaches into his mailbox.

Call him at any time of the day or night. Criticize him on the telephone and attempt to influence him politically. He will have to accept the calls whether he wants to or not since he never knows if it is a call from his office or headquarters. To hear night after night that one "will be picked up" and that "one will receive the bill for payment" will tear even the strongest nerves of a traitor.

c. How to make his life more difficult in still other ways:

A mailman should damage his mail on purpose (letters, newspapers get wet or wadded up and partially torn; let packages fall into the mud).

Laundry personnel should not wash his clothes clean or iron them nicely. Pour bleach into the wash water so that clothes will suffer unduly. If you don't have these means, leave his clothes in the washing machine three or four times as long as required.

If you are unfortunate enough to be a forced laborer in one of his laundries, you can harass the enemy most by excessive use of soap and soap powder. They are items always short in supply, thus rationed. Insufficient rinsing will soon lead to chemical damages. Ironing with a very hot iron will affect linen adversely. But watch out! Too much heat will brown the material and thus betray your intentions. Here, the same as any other place, the main problem is that one can "blunder" only to the extent that merchandise or a piece of work will just slip by in case of a check.

Doctors, pharmacists, druggists, nurses, etc.

The above will treat and supply medicine to people who have joined the underground.

Always give the appearance of using more medicine and medical supplies than is really needed. Put aside the "surplus" and have it transported secretly to the guerrilla units via the resistance movement.

Warehousemen (food warehouses, fuel depots, etc.)

Distribute goods located in the central depots. Prior to arrival of occupation troops, distribute food and fuel to the civilian population. Otherwise the enemy will seize the depots and use them for his troops and/or industry.

The individual housewife will be able to easily hide the small portion given her.

Administration officials

Perform each job in as complicated and time-consuming manner as possible. Increase the use of office materials. Misplace, hide or destroy personnel records.

Frequently interrupt telephone conversations with members of the occupation force by hanging up on them. Only call back after five or ten minutes and excuse yourself profusely, explaining that you had been cut off.

Word directives and orders ambiguously. Cause controversy over the competence of employees.

Personnel officials

Cause personnel lists to disappear. By doing this you will make it difficult for the enemy to make up lists of persons to be used for forced labor and deported, or to ascertain degrees of relationship during the arrest of clans and arrest of hostages. Execution or deportation of family members, relatives or acquaintances in place of fugitive assailants or saboteurs).

Town officials

Town officials can steal blank identification cards. ID cards manufactured and issued by the enemy cannot be stolen by the thousands during an opportune moment. Otherwise you will run the risk that the occupation power will void the entire issue; thus your efforts and risks taken may have been in vain. Police officials and town administrations must, therefore, put aside continuously small quantities (three to four pieces at one time) so that the loss will be unnoticed. By means of a liaison man they are then passed on to the resistance movement which, in turn, will pass them on to the counterfeit section for "processing."

Passports, personal ID cards of any type, identification papers, etc., of deceased persons may under no circumstances be returned to the issuing office even if this is required by regulation. If necessary, make up excuses. For instance, you did not see one or the deceased has never mentioned the existence of such a document. The enemy will be unable to check on these statements; the dead are silent for ever.

Pass all these documents on to the resistance movement which can use them as a basis for new documents (change of names, dates, stamps, photos and description by the counterfeit section).

The need for counterfeit documents is enormous to provide "cover" for those who have gone "underground."

Uniformed Railroad Officials

Give one of your uniforms to the resistance movement. It will allow them to conduct railroad sabotage more inconspicuously if disguised as railroad employees (easier approach of targets, better chances to reconnoitre). Label freight cars incorrectly. Direct freight cars to the wrong destinations. Load and unload cars slowly. "Forget" where cars are located.

Uniformed postal, telegraph and telephone officials (for instance, mailmen).

Give one of your uniforms to the resistance movement. Disguised as mailmen, they will be able to place underground newspapers, leaflets, etc, in the mailboxes of clients without causing suspicion.

In addition, people disguised in uniform are better able to approach telephone switchboards, etc., to commit sabotage.

Postal employees

Postal employees can "lose" official mail, forward official mail to wrong addresses or intentionally delay or re-address official mail.

Bank employee

Bank employees can spread the rumor that a currency reform is imminent. The ensuing wave of purchases and accompanying disturbances of all types will be of great nuisance to the enemy.

Telephone operator at switch boards

Do not take calls from offices of the occupation troops. Make bad connections so that they can only be established with effort which will cause general annoyance. Disrupt connections in the middle of conversations. If necessary you can always make up some sort of excuse ("technical defect").

Police officials (Search personnel and uniformed policemen)

General:

The enemy will attempt to take over in its entirety the existing local police organizations and use them for his purposes. Primarily, the local police will: regulate traffic the same as before; fight against crime (common criminals, not political "criminals"); continue the administration of penal installations containing criminals.

Independent from the local police forces, the occupation power will institute its own police apparatus for the political sector by organizing the State Security Service and an informer net.

The enemy will establish prisons and concentration camps for political prisoners ("State enemy," "Terrorists," "Peoples' Enemies," "unteachable grumblers," as they are so beautifully described in his terminology).

However, the enemy higher police headquarters will always use the local police for certain missions and support—depending upon his estimate of the degree of reliability of the local police force. This will happen especially in the criminalistic field since the State Security Service will possess only limited capabilities and is composed more of sadists than of criminologists.

During this forced and repetitious cooperation of our former security and criminal investigation police force with those of the enemy a series of possibilities exist for sabotage.

Possibilities for sabotage:

a. For uniformed policemen

As a member of a selected corps, knowing weapons and well trained physically, you should belong to a guerrilla detachment where you can render good services. If for special reasons you have not been able to join one of these detachments, act as follows:

(1) Warn persons you are to arrest or of whose imminent arrest you have knowledge.

(2) Give one of your uniforms to the resistance movement. Phony policemen, disguised in uniforms, can obtain entrance to a prison, for instance, and get our arrested resistance fighters "legally."

(3) During fire fights with saboteurs or fugitive political prisoners, your weapon will jam or you will be unable to hit anyone. You can claim that you always have been a poor shot.

You also can quickly run out of ammunition. Hide the majority of ammunition you are carrying with you.

At an opportune moment during fire fights, fire in the backs of the enemy police or military elements with whom you have to cooperate. Afterwards, the enemy will hardly find out by whose bullets his personnel were killed. With his well known ruthlessness, it is unlikely that his own people will be that valuable to him.

During an engagement, fire upon your own parked vehicles—squad, prison, and radio cars. For it is impossible to prove that it was your own bullets and not those of the enemy.

Sabotage, for instance. cordons by pretending not to pay attention which will allow the break-out of encircled resistance fighters.

Collect ammunition at any opportune moment so that you will have a large private cache when you join a guerrilla detachment.

Possibilities:

When on patrol open fire upon imagined saboteurs. But only fire two to three rounds to cause the weapon to become dirty; afterward you will clean it at the police station while complaining. Retain five or six rounds as "expended" and hide them. Your patrol partner can vouch for the fire fight. In addition, shots were heard.

During larger engagements in which you participate, expend almost no ammunition at all and retain it and hand grenades. Also attempt to hide weapons.

In cooperation with doctors have them issue false certificates of accidents so that injured resistance fighters can be legally admitted to a hospital and treated disguised as "victims of traffic."

b. Drivers of police vehicles

As driver of a police vehicle you will make your vehicle temporarily available to the resistance movement. A police car is an ideal vehicle to transport weapons, ammunition, explosives, leaflets, underground newspapers, radios, etc. There is no better cover than a police vehicle.

Persons in danger who cannot expose themselves in public any more can be inconspicuously transported to safety and are relatively safe by posing as prisoners.

There will be many times when you are alone in the vehicle and, consequently, will be able to use it to aid the resistance movement. Your efforts will be facilitated if your colleagues and superiors ignore your activities.

If you have to drive your squad car with a single detachment into operation against the underground, sabotage the operation by a variety of means. Pretend to have difficulty in starting the engine. Take a circuitous route to the objective or get lost. You may claim that the blackout confused you. Have a minor accident by running into a light pole or a telephone pole, or fire hydrant. The blackout can serve again as an excuse.

c. Prison warden

Allow political prisoners to escape whenever this can be done without attracting attention.

If you notice that people possessing false passes, ID cards and orders, want to pick up political prisoners, look the other way.

At a later period, you may deem it necessary to join a guerrilla detachment or to go completely "underground" with the resistance movement in order to avoid being arrested. Before leaving, allow the political prisoners to escape.

Make a wax impression of the keys. But do not take the keys along otherwise the enemy will change the locks. The resistance movement will be grateful for the wax impressions. Take along as many weapons, ammunition and uniforms as you possibly can.

d. Police radio operator

Inform the resistance movement of everything of interest to them which you may have been able to monitor.

If, at some given point, you have to go "underground," attempt to take equipment along. If necessary, help stage a raid by members of the resistance movement who will be disguised as policemen. The real officials who will only pretend to resist.

e. Criminal investigation personnel

Remove incriminating evidence from the scene of acts of sabotage or assassination attempts.

Mislead elements of the enemy State Security Service. For instance, blame the incident on a traitor who will then be neutralized. Misplace, steal and destroy any evidence. Warn persons who become suspects.

Priests

Destroy or hide all lists of religious groups and associations in your possession; otherwise they will be used by the enemy to draw up lists of individuals to be held as hostages and to be deported.

If activities such as church services, baptism rites, communion, confirmation, etc., are prohibited by the new dictators—which will happen for certain sooner or later—take up a "fictitious profession." The most desirable cover would be one which would allow you to travel a great deal such as an errand boy, a meter reader for gas and electric companies, fund raiser for any organization, an insurnce agent, etc.

You will thus be able to continue your ministry "under cover" simply by visiting the people individually instead of having them come to your church. They will also feed you and support your family so that you will be able to select the "fictitious profession" based on above rules without having to take into consideration the salary.

Kindergarten nurses, teachers

Without doubt you will have the most difficult task. On one

hand instruction material such as new school books and schedules are strictly regulated and supervised by the occupying powers, and on the other hand you are in a key position in which you should sabotage enemy efforts more than anyone else. This is a fight for the mind of the youth. I can give you little advice at this time.

Enemy efforts will concentrate primarily in the following areas:

(1) Children will be instructed to report any unfriendly remarks made about the regime. The final goal is to have an informer (the child) in each family so that parents and sisters and brothers will be watched. Possible counter-measures: Emphasize and cultivate the family's feeling of loyalty to one another.

(2) Attempts will be made to misrepresent and change history.

(3) Efforts will be made to degrade and neutralize all former democratic institutions and principles.

(4) The enemy will supplant instruction in citizenship with his own ideology and party doctrine.

(5) All instruction such as reading, writing, arithmetic, history, geography, etc., will be systematically saturated with politics. The first words which the young student will spell or write will be party slogans of the enemy.

(6) Such words as peace, freedom, democracy will be so twisted and distorted that the younger generation will no longer know what they really mean.

(7) The occupation power will force students to learn its language.

(8) Religion will be ridiculed. Attempts will be made to disprove religious beliefs by dishonest presentation of scientific fact.

(9) A personality cult will be developed and nurtured.

Counter such measures by cultivating the ability to judge critically and emphasizing human values, such as loyalty, friendship, readiness to help.

I am fully aware that I did not offer many concrete solutions. However, with mere general phrases you are not offered any help. As mentioned above, this is the most difficult and almost the most important problem. It therefore stands to reason that you should think about these questions thoroughly and discuss them with colleagues. Perhaps you will find the solutions which I am unable to offer here. A group often finds a solution more easily than an individual.

Engineers and technicians in industrial plants

Make mistakes during construction. Institute changes at the onset of mass production. Mismanage the supply of spare parts.

Employees in plants and shops

Work slowly. Turn out poor quality goods and produce many rejects. Take a break often. Treat machinery, installations and engines carelessly. Cause excessive waste. Use excessive quantities of water, power, fuel and grease. Take excessive sick leave.

Engineers, architects, and builders

Make excessively high estimates of materials needed which are in short supply such as cement, reinforcing rods, etc. Charge the highest prices possible. Extend construction periods as long as possible. Cooperate with your colleagues in this effort.

Construction workers

If you have to build fortifications, obstacles, billets, roads, etc., for the enemy, you will be able to mix in considerably more cement than necessary for the requirement can be calculated exactly. Cement is always in short supply and a systematic great increase in consumption would inevitably lead to shortages for the enemy. On the other hand, you can reduce the quality of the product by adding too little cement.

When putting insufficient quantities of cement into the concrete to weaken the structure, throw the remaining cement away in order to give the appearance of having used up the calculated amount and to preclude a reduction in amount of cement allocated for the project. Work as negligently, slowly, and poorly as possible.

Taxi drivers

Always use a circuitous route to get to the destination to cause the enemy the greatest loss in time and highest cost possible. Pretend not to be familiar with the route.

When enemy personnel indicate they are in a hurry to make a train or attend a meeting, fake a breakdown and cause him to be late.

Streetcar conductors and bus drivers

Close the doors in front of the nose of occupation personnel and their followers when they attempt to enter. Ignore enemy personnel waiting at bus stops. Keep on driving. Ignore the enemy's signals to stop the streetcar or bus when he wants off. Your fellow citizens will gladly walk back or wait for the next bus or streetcar if the enemy can be harrassed.

Vehicle mechanic

There are many ways in which you can impair the effectiveness of the enemy's vehicles. Set the engine to increase gasoline consumption. When changing oil, secretly fill the crankcase with old oil. Fill radiator with insufficient amount of anti-freeze. Make out oil and grease tickets incorrectly so as to cause increased oil and grease consumption or usage of the vehicle. Grease vehicle badly or not at all.

Gas station attendent

Throw sugar into the gas tank which will result in a breakdown, search for cause of breakdown, and an unpleasant repair job.

When filling tanks out of separate canisters, pour diesel oil into gasoline-operated vehicles and vice versa. This results in breakdown, unpleasant repair jobs. As an excuse, you can say you simply made a mistake in the cans. When checking tires, put in too much or too little air. In one case the wear of tires will increase, in the other the suspension system will be strained too much.

Artisan

When you are called up for a repair job, pretend you have too much work on hand and put off the job as long as possible. Only use inferior material. Charge an exhorbitant price.

Owners of radio shops

All radios will be confiscated by the enemy sooner or later. Consequently, you must put aside a stock of spare parts which will be needed by the resistance movement and guerrilla units.

Hide all portable radios; this can be easily done due to their small size. Also stock up on batteries for the same.

Salesgirls in grocery stores

Intentionally overlook members of the occupation forces and collaborators to cause them to complain in order to be served at all. If you have to answer for your behavior, present profuse excuses in order to repeat the same tactics with the next member.

Make a point to give them the worst of everything, such as partially rotten fruit, vegetables, salads and the smallest pieces of meat, bread, etc.

Intentionally damage any merchandise he requests. Squeeze fruit before packing it. Put down paper bag heavily on counter, so that fruit will be bruised and therefore spoil quickly.

Salesgirls in department stores

Sell him impractical articles such as souvenirs, watches, jewelry, clothes, shoes, etc. Sell him damaged or faulty merchandise or objects. Damage merchandise or objects he buys prior to packing them. For instance cut into a piece of cloth, put grease or paint on it. Assert that certain items he asks for are no longer in stock. If he proves the contrary, indicate you are sorry you made a mistake.

Catering business

(1) Waiters and waitresses in hotels, restaurants

Continue to ignore the enemy so that he has to complain in order to be served at all. Take his order as inattentively, slowly and indifferently as possible. Always give him the worst of everything such as the worst wine at the highest price, etc.

(2) Owner

Encourage your personnel to act as outlined above by ignoring complaints of the enemy. Assign foreign military personel or traitors the worst rooms you can.

There are problems and dangers for artisans and shop owners, butchers, bakers, department stores, tailors, shoe repairmen, repair shops, who harass the enemy in ways mentioned above.

All of the above procedures of passive resistance will only be successful when all shop owners and artisans cooperate so that the enemy or his followers cannot simply run to a competitor.

You must all present one solid front. He who fails to cooperate with this front because of greed shall be considered a collaborator and will be called to account for his actions after liberation.

The temptation for the individual to profit greatly by this "voluntary elimination" of competition and to be the only one to do a lucrative business is very great.

The resistance movement must clearly explain to these egotists that such activity is treason and that nothing will be forgotten nor forgiven.

Farmers

In the "occupied" area, a delivery quota will be very quickly imposed. Deliveries of grain, potatoes, fruit, dairy products, pigs and cattle can be estimated accurately which will prevent you from concealing almost anything at all. However, overproduce as much as possible in other sectors such as garden vegetables, sheep, goats, chickens and rabbits.

Use these surplus products for the guerrilla units as well as for personnel gone "underground." The finance section of the resistance movement as well as headquarters of guerrilla units will pay you as much as they possibly can.

In temporarily "liberated" areas deliver the entire harvest voluntarily to guerrilla detachments. It is better to have it in the hands of our own people than to have the enemy profit by it. If you don't, everything will be confiscated by the enemy under the pretext "of having helped the partisans" once the guerrilla units are forced to leave and your area becomes enemy occupied territory again.

Retain only what you need for yourself (self-supply, seeds for coming year.) You can always claim that the harvest was taken away by force by the partisans.

Harvest time is also time for a "major offensive" by the guerrilla units who will attempt to liberate as large and as rich an area as possible to prevent the enemy from getting the harvest and at the same time increasing their own supply for the coming winter.

It is obvious, of course, that you must assist in these efforts. If your area is under enemy occupation, slow down the harvest in hopes that a guerrilla unit will arrive in time to take the grain or produce from the enemy.

Speed up the harvest if you are in a "liberated" area so that it can be stored and the surplus given to guerrilla units so that they can hide it before the enemy begins a counter-offensive.

Make your own transportation means available—horses, tractors, carts—to transport harvest surpluses to guerrilla caches and depots.

"Infiltration" of Armed Party Organizations

The enemy will soon create an armed factory militia in important industrial plants, the transportation system and administration.

In their effort to create a "mass organization" and to flatter the foreign dictator and master with impressive figures, the new powers will be unable to find sufficient members really true to the party line. Consequently, they will be forced to fill their thin ranks with many others less dedicated and politically reliable.

Here you will find great opportunities to infiltrate the enemy organization.

Leading positions as well as members of crew-served weapons will, based on past experience, always be filled by absolutely dependable party members, whereas the unreliable will be assigned lower missions such as ammunition bearer, rifle men, etc.

By infiltrating members of the resistance movement into these armed fighting organizations of the party, you will be able to do the following during a decisive hour:

(1) Dispose of weapons and ammunition;
(2) Reduce the fighting strength of these units by mediocre cooperation;
(3) Be informed of their measures and thus reveal and thwart them;
(4) Shoot the "party fanatics" in the back at an opportune moment and then join the population.

Final remarks

During passive resistance the individual needle prick is useless as such. However, thousands such pricks together will create unbearable conditions for the enemy. The decisive factor is to unite the citizenry and to maintain resistance over a long period.

Each time you are able to perform a jabbing operation you will feel a small triumph and notice that after all you are not so defenseless. These small personal victories will increase your fighting spirit and will to resist.

Do not forget the first and foremost rule: "Seek connections with and support of persons thinking the same as you. He who is lonely and isolated will lose his belief in his own strength and in the victory of the good cause."

The enemy will be in a position, of course, to make passive resistance more difficult by increased control. However, he will be unable to eliminate it completely. Only when a supervisor is placed behind each working member will the enemy be able to forestall this resistance. And even then you succeed.

17. Sabotage

During sabotage it is of importance to be able to get to the heart of the installation. The simplest way is to obtain a suitable job. Sometimes you will be able to influence workers to carry out sabotage, other times you will have to infiltrate members of the resistance movement into the target area.

Individuals in administrative and office capacities can best hinder the enemy by a "slowdown" campaign. This is relatively safe. The work pace is simply reduced drastically automatically causing a reduction in the production output.

In highly industrialized, automated plants where the pulse and tempo of the production process are dictated by the machine, so to speak, delaying tactics are difficult to apply. On the other hand, you will find many opportunities to sabotage machinery, and instruments.

A small breakdown will bring the entire highly complicated production process to a standstill.

General sabotage possibilities

Activate air raid sirens through sabotage. The false alarm will have everyone running to air raid shelters and will interrupt the entire public life for hours. After the all clear signal, you will then return slowly to your job in order to waste as much time as possible.

Take advantage of a chaos after air raids. After air raids you will be able to destroy important machinery and appliances which

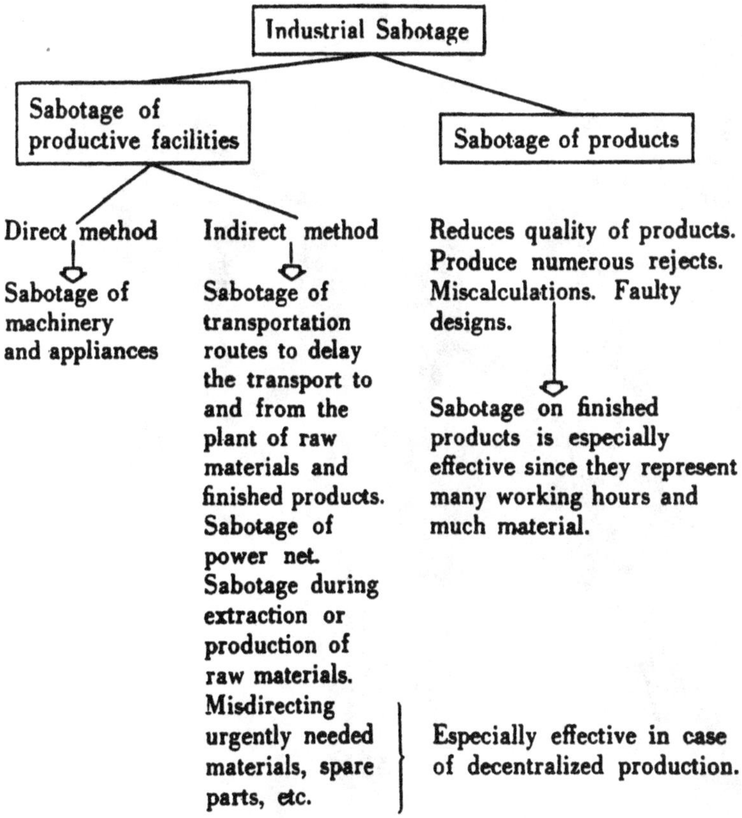

Industrial sabotage

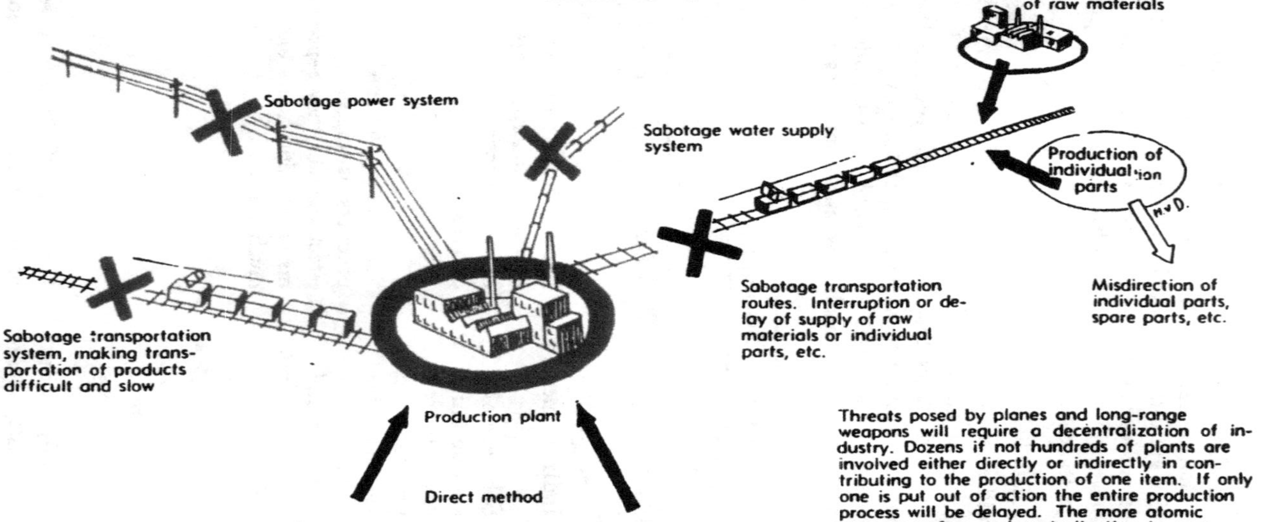

Sabotage machinery and appliances
Rescheduling when mass production is about to begin
Create disputes as to who is competent, etc.
Miscalculations and faulty designs, etc.

Threats posed by planes and long-range weapons will require a decentralization of industry. Dozens if not hundreds of plants are involved either directly or indirectly in contributing to the production of one item. If only one is put out of action the entire production process will be delayed. The more atomic weapons enfore a decentralization in rear areas, the more the production will become vulnerable to sabotage. Even in this secondary area, modern weapons increase the effectiveness of guerrilla warfare, as paradoxical as it may sound. Atomic weapons increase the value of the partisan and the resistance fighter.

have survived the attack. You can do this during the general confusion under the cover of attempting to render assistance. You thus will be able to get to important targets which normally are out of your reach. Demolition and fire fighting personnel of the resistance movement are able to carry out missions of destruction during and after heavy night bombing attacks.

They may disguise themselves in uniform or coveralls of the fire department and civil air defense organization. These missions will go unnoticed and thus unpunished in the general chaos. Raids and attacks can also be conducted at this favorable time.

Prisons that have been damaged can be attacked by raiding patrols of the resistance movement to free the prisoners.

18. Raids Conducted by the Civilian Resistance Movement.

In certain exceptional cases the resistance movement will have to resort to raids. It may be necessary to free imprisoned resistance fighters from police stations, interrogation cellars and, if necessary, even prisons if the danger exists that they might reveal important facts under torture. It also may be necessary to free hostages, capture files or destroy key industrial installations and transportation facilities.

Organization of Raid:

Phase One: Preparations

Since the State Security Service will search for the participants of the raid, all must have an alibi for staying away from work without attracting attention or suspicion. Pretending to be ill is the best way. Symptoms of illness reported to the office of a plant by coworkers must later coincide with the doctor's report issued by a doctor belonging to the underground movement.

In a larger city the sewage system will have to be prepared as a hiding place should things go wrong. It should be stocked with food, beverages, first aid equipment, extra clothes, ammunition, maps, etc.

A detailed reconnaissance of target area must be performed. Routes of withdrawal must be designated and prepared.

Phase Two:

Fire support elements must take over houses neighboring the target. For this purpose apartments and shops may have to be rented. If necessary, fire support elements may have to occupy these places several days before the operation and live there.

Disassembled submachine guns, light machine guns, assault guns, pistols, hand grenades and ammunition can be transported to the selected positions in briefcases, tool boxes, or suitcases.

A courier service must be organized; women, young boys and girls are especially suited for this job.

The raiding party conducting the operation can benefit from the black-out. Anyone still on the street after curfew is automatically considered an enemy. The raiding party will wear shoes with rubber soles, dark clothes and will blacken face and hands.

By virtue of the fact that the population has to stay inside after curfew, you may use your weapons more ruthlessly than during the day since no innocent people will be on the streets.

During the day, the raiding party will best be loaded onto a covered truck and will then drive directly in front of the target. When the raiding party detrucks, this will automatically signal for fire support elements to open fire from their prepared positions.

Possible methods of sealing of routes of access to target area:

Resistance members pose as street cleaners. "Street cleaners" can be used in an excellent manner as security guards; they will hide submachine guns and hand grenades in their carts; or else you can use "mechanics" carrying their weapons in their tool boxes.

Block routes of access by simulating a traffic accident. The driver involved can escape in the confusion created in this manner. The "accident," which will take place when the raiding party has opened fire, will prevent police from arriving too soon. The driver, should he be apprehended, can explain that he was scared and thus caused the accident.

Phase Three: Withdrawal

Plans will have to include provisions for withdrawal after a successful operation or discontinuation of operation if the target cannot be reached. Concealed personnel with submachine guns, mines and prepared road blocks will be used to keep routes of withdrawal open. It may be necessary to disappear in the sewer system and wait until the search operation, which may go on for several days, has been discontinued.

Methods of covering withdrawal:

If you use motor vehicles you must install armor in back of the driver's seat to prevent the driver from being hit by bullets from pursuing vehicles. Since only light weapons, i.e., pistols, submachine guns and perhaps automatic rifles, and no armor piercing bullets will be used, a steel plate about 10 millimeters thick will suffice. Install several sand bags or perhaps an additional low steel plate 10 millimeters thick and 50 to 60 centimeters high at the rear end of the truck to protect personnel lying on the floor. Pursuing elements can be discouraged with hand grenades and submachine guns.

You may establish road blocks along the planned routes of approach. Members of the resistance movement on road blocks, may use a variety of methods to stop your pursuers.

Raid conducted by party of the resistance movement.

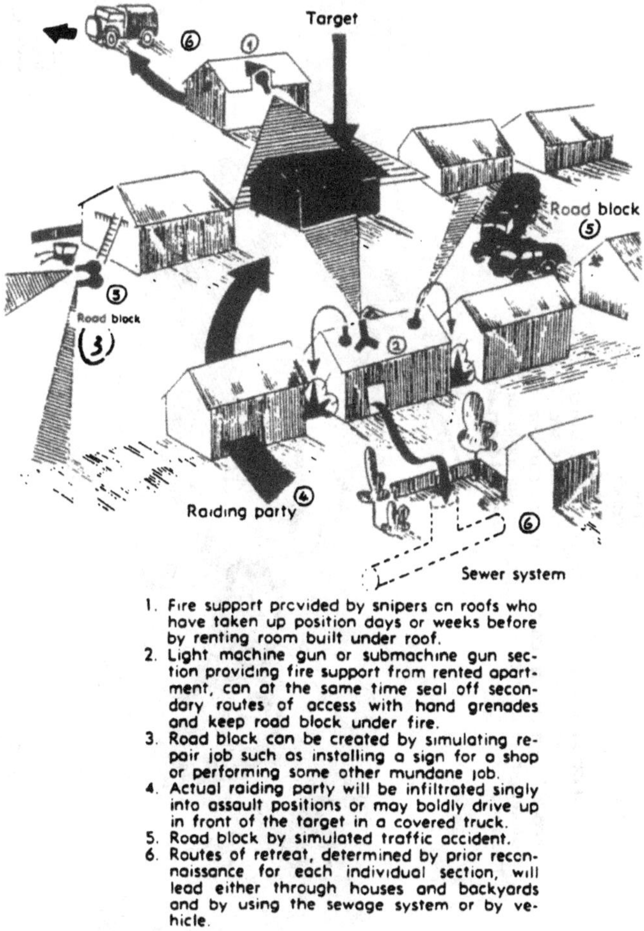

1. Fire support provided by snipers on roofs who have taken up position days or weeks before by renting room built under roof.
2. Light machine gun or submachine gun section providing fire support from rented apartment, can at the same time seal off secondary routes of access with hand grenades and keep road block under fire.
3. Road block can be created by simulating repair job such as installing a sign for a shop or performing some other mundane job.
4. Actual raiding party will be infiltrated singly into assault positions or may boldly drive up in front of the target in a covered truck.
5. Road block by simulated traffic accident.
6. Routes of retreat, determined by prior reconnaissance for each individual section, will lead either through houses and backyards and by using the sewage system or by vehicle.

Covering the withdrawal after the raid.

1. Establish road block by blasting a tree.
2. Road block by board with mines pushed across the street.
3. A loaded vehicle or cart is placed in middle of the road.
4. Activate trip wire to stake mines along side of road.
5. Throw out hand grenades and submachine gun fire from the vehicle.
6. Makeshift armor in back of driver's seat and sandbags or armor in front of the tail gate protects personnel from enemy fire.

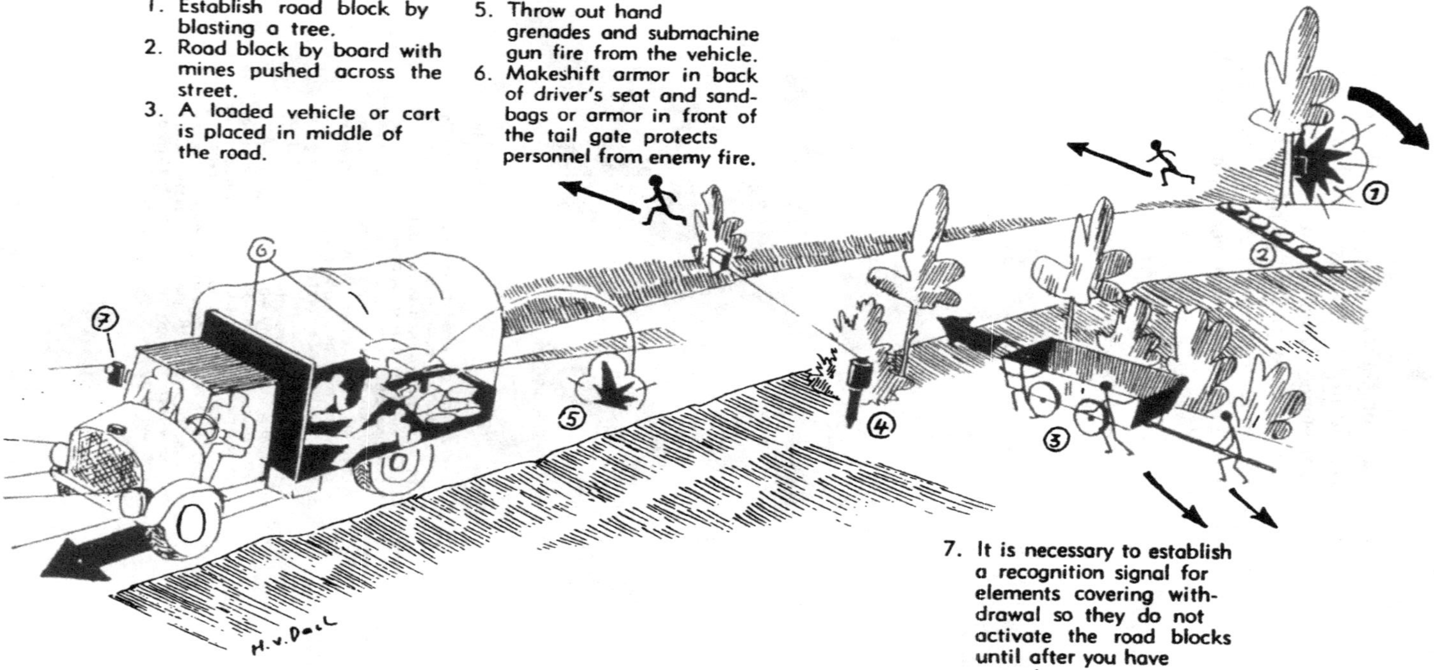

7. It is necessary to establish a recognition signal for elements covering withdrawal so they do not activate the road blocks until after you have passed.

After you have passed they can string a steel cable across the street, push a cart in the road, or open fire and then disappear. Mines, laid and camouflaged the day before, can be activated.

Trees can be dropped across the road. Blast a tree across the street.

In order for personnel manning these road blocks to be able to recognize your vehicle at night from those of the enemy, you must agree upon a sign, i.e., a red flashlight shining from the driver's seat, etc.

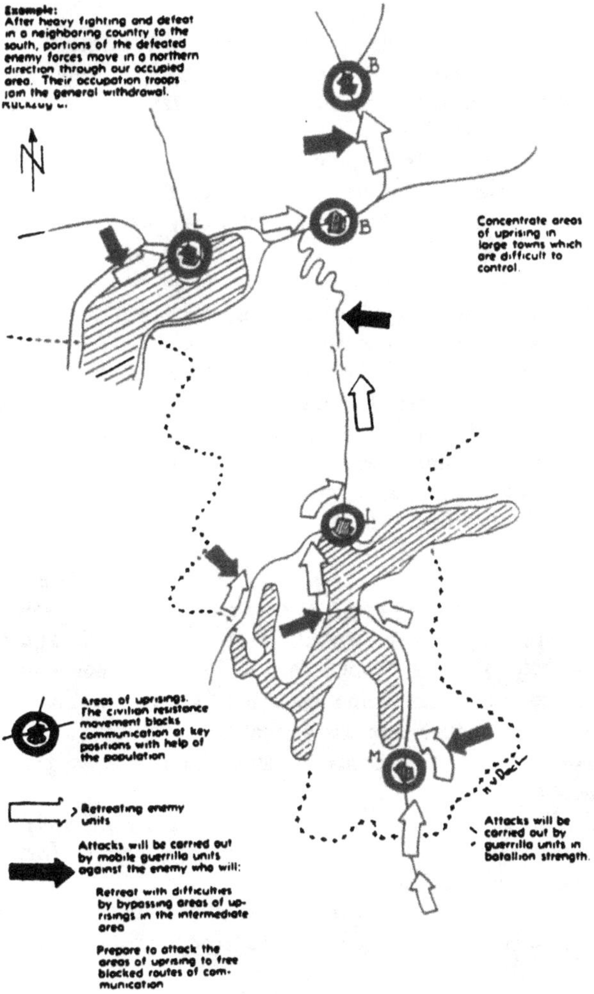

Booby trapping the road block will cause the enemy losses, assuming he can stop in time to clear the obstacle. He will suffer more casualties from booby traps than usual since being in hot pursuit and wanting to clear the street quickly he will be careless.

19. The Last Phase of Resistance: General Uprising.

The revolt of the Maquis in France (especially Paris) with the approach of the allies and of the Polish underground forces led by General Bor in Warsaw are good historical examples of a mass uprising.

A general uprising speeds up the collapse of the enemy.

Success depends upon the selection of the right time. If you initiate the attack too soon, the uprising will fail. If you act too late you will miss your chance.

The moment for general uprising arrives when the enemy has been put on the defensive by events far away. Your efforts will be assisted by the approaching allied armies who may provide assistance, by the enemy sending some occupation units elsewhere or by his voluntarily withdrawing from your area.

In addition to advantages of a purely technical nature, such as preventing large scale destruction, dismantling of industry, etc., open uprisings will provide you with other advantages which should not be underestimated. For instance, your position in regards to the world political situation and likelihood of maintaining the sovereignty of your country will be much better after the war if you are able to reconquer large portions of your country yourself, rather than waiting passively for liberation and salvation by foreign countries.

With a little luck you may be able to get by with indirect help during the liberation campaign such as air support, supply of weapons and ammunition, etc., provided by allied armies and thus you may not need the help of their ground forces. This way you can also prevent your country from being occupied again even though by friendly forces. Past experience shows that even "allies" and "liberators" cannot be removed so easily. At least, it's harder to get them to leave than to enter.

And finally, at the end of the war, you will immediately have your own army again, even though primitive, which will form the basis for a new, better force.

During the phase of the "open uprising" the civilian resistance movement will serve as the stationary, local troops of the towns especially for key traffic installations, whereas the guerrilla units will serve as the mobile fighting forces.

The idea is to block the enemy's internal routes of communication and route of withdrawal by open insurrection of the population and to smash the enemy retreating in the intermediate area or getting ready to free the blocked communication routes with the mobile guerrilla units.

It is obvious, of course, that maximum use has to be made of the terrain. Concentrate uprisings in large towns and cities which will be difficult for the enemy to suppress. Mobile guerrilla forces in the intermediate area will attack at favorable terrain features such as ravines, so that the enemy will be unable to utilize his superior force or at least not be able to commit them at the same time. Mobile units should conduct attacks in at least batallion strength.

Even though fighting in unfavorable terrain, the enemy must be under attack from two sides. For instance, if he is attempting to suppress an insurrection in a city, guerrilla units should attack his flanks or rear.

Tactics of uprising

a. Preparations:

Procure a lot of city maps for yourself and your subordinate leaders. During city fighting they play the same role as maps for operations in the open terrain.

At important tactical places you must lease apartments, shops or even houses where you can take up position long beforehand, i.e., at bridges, intersections, train stations, telephone offices, exit routes, etc.

Make a reconnaissance of church steeples and high houses which can be used as observation posts. Prepare and camouflage them. For instance, install telephone lines which will only require connecting during the hour of decision.

At important locations you can prepare cellar windows, etc., as machine gun and anti-tank positions and camouflage them. For instance, install weapons racks at appropriate height to support weapons. Obtain sand bags to stabilize tripods or bipods or to reinforce walls. At the last moment all you have to do is place the weapons in position.

In this manner you already have some trumps in your hands when the uprising breaks out.

b. Occupation of town:

Similar procedures will be used as mentioned in the chapter on

"Tactics of Guerrilla Units." However, here the difference is that the participants in this case are members of "fighting groups" of the civilian resistance movement and not of the guerrilla units. In addition, depots, munition and arms factories will also have to be occupied.

c. Defense of towns:

You must primarily anticipate counter-attacks by tanks. The mobile reserve units of the occupation forces consist mostly of mechanized police regiments with attached tank elements.

Seal off communications within the town. The enemy will thus be able to make use of his superior means—artillery, tanks, planes—only on a restricted scale.

Your forces will be such—even with complete assistance of the entire population—that you will be unable to occupy all buildings. Militarily speaking this is not necessary. Establish strong points at the most important traffic junctions, bridges, train stations, intersection of main routes, etc. The area in between the individual strong points will be patrolled by combat patrols.

Conduct large-scale reconnaissance all over town at all times by using the civilian population—especially women, young boys and girls. As a result, you will never be surprised by the enemy.

Form a main reserve unit and motorize it with trucks, captured armored personnel carriers.

Distribution of forces available:

Personnel (armed fighters); ¼ at strong points, ¼ in raiding parties, ½ in main reserve.

Ammunition and weapons:

1. At strong points:

Concentrate all machine guns, snipers, Molotov cocktails, explosives and mines for anti-tank defense, approximately 1/5 of ammunition available, approximately 1/5 of hand grenades on hand.

2. Raiding parties:

They should possess the majority of submachine guns and anti-tank weapons, approximately 1/5 of ammunition available, approximately 3/5 of hand grenades available, and all anti-tank or rifle grenades.

3. Main reserve:

Main reserve should have all captured AP carriers and tanks, all light machine guns and rocket launchers, approximately 3/5 of ammunition available, and approximately 1/5 of hand grenades available.

If the enemy bypasses these strong points and reroutes traffic via secondary streets through a town, act as follows:

Install individual, well camouflaged snipers on roofs, top floors and rooms located up high. Practically invisible and out of reach, they can disturb the rerouted enemy traffic with well-aimed fire.

Conduct reconnaissances with the aid of the population. Infiltrate through these gaps with raiding parties to get to the bypasses.

Consolidation of strong points:

Use the population to help you. Your greatest trump is the mass utilization of desperate human masses to give the last they have. With their help you will be able to convert your strong points into fortresses in a period of hours rather than days.

Work plans, lists of material, order of priority for various projects and supervisory personnel for the work forces have to be determined down to the smallest detail prior to the uprising.

The masses of people not belonging to the active fighting groups of the resistance movement must fill sand bags. They can use jute bags and fill them with dirt, sand, etc.

Install wire meshing in basement and first-floor windows of houses to be used as strong points against hand grenades.

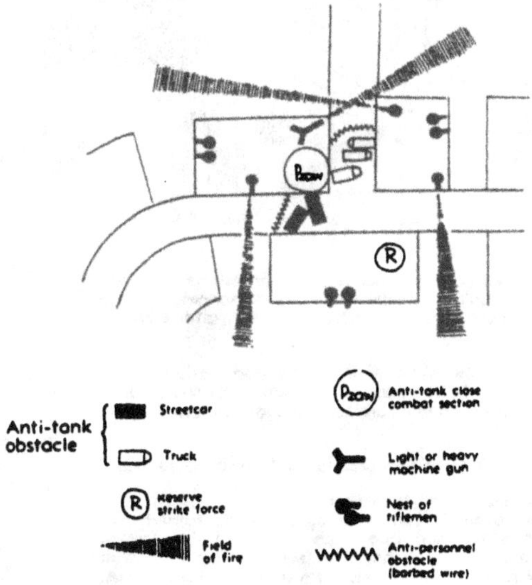

Internal organization of anti-tank obstacle within the strong point.

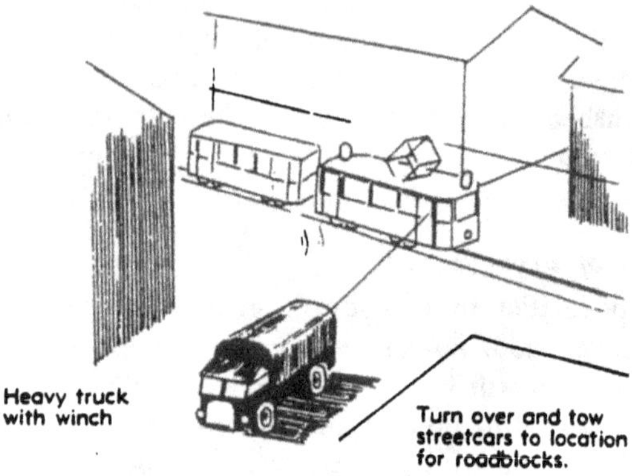

1. Personnel with hand grenades and submachine guns defend anti-tank obstacle and anti-personnel obstacle against enemy tank-mounted infantry and engineer personnel.

2. Personnel throw Molotov cocktails and perhaps anti-tank gunners fight tanks and assault guns should they become "bold" and "careless" enough to drive up to the obstacle.

3. Snipers watch over surrounding roofs and house walls.

4. Anti-tank close combat section.
   Anti-tank obstacle consisting of streetcars turned over or vehicles rammed into each other will be erected behind a corner of a house in such a way so that it is out of range of tank guns from a long distance; thus, the enemy will be forced to remove the obstacle using infantry personnel whether he wants to or not.

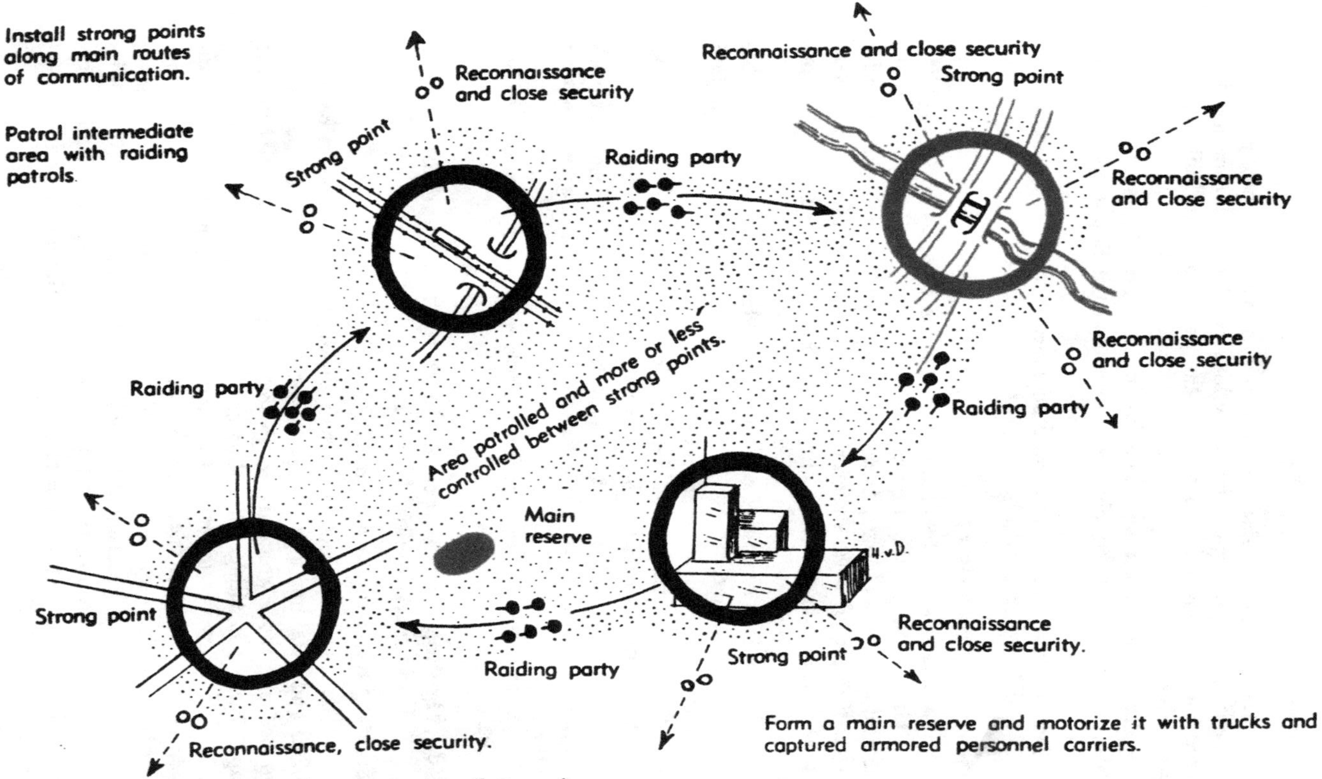

Organization of city defense during general uprising.

Erect anti-tank obstacles utilizing street cars, heavy vehicles, cement pipes, pneumatic drills, bulldozers. Requisition cranes from construction companies to tear up the pavement and build up piles of rubble.

Erect anti-personnel obstacles made out of fences and barbed wire. Material can be obtained from construction companies and stores.

Stock ammunition and food supplies at the strong points.

Fill Molotov cocktails.

Internal organization of strong points:

Each strong point will consist of two or three buildings together.

Only occupy buildings of solid construction such as schools, administration buildings, factories, etc. Avoid modern brick buildings. Reinforced steel structures or older houses (author refers to stone houses common in Switzerland) best withstand the fire from tank guns.

The various buildings composing the strong points must be able to give each other fire support and together control an important point such as bridges, road intersection, or square.

The tank obstacle must be installed in such a manner so as to be able to be covered by the entire strong point organization.

Your field of fire must be such that at least two sides of each occupied building can be covered by fire from the neighboring house.

A small reserve force of four to five men belongs in each strong point.

20. Fighting Techniques Utilized by the Superior Enemy While Surpressing Uprisings.

Entering towns in the area of the uprising

The enemy will select primarily the early morning hours between 0200 and 0400 hours. The last "night revellers" will then have gone to bed and those who have to go to the early shift have not yet got up. Towns and villages are thus surprised "in bed" so to speak.

If for any reason at all the morning hours cannot be taken advantage of, for instance, transportation difficulties, he will select the late forenoon hours (1000-1100) when the masses are at work.

While he is entering, the civilian telephone system will be disrupted to prevent you from reporting his strength, organization and direction of advance via the civilian net to your underground movement.

Siege—Martial law

Immediately after entry into the area of unrest the enemy will declare martial law. You also must know something about this so as not to be surprised and impressed too much.

a. Taking over command:

A military command will take over in place of the civilian occupation administration or the "puppet administration" and will institute the following:

b. Individual measures:

Restaurants and clubs will be forced to close before dusk.

Curfew at night. In his own interest the enemy has to issue "passes" valid for the curfew hours to doctors as well as employees most needed in public installations such as gas works, power works, water supply, hospitals, etc. By clever falsifications you may be able to get a hold of such passes and thus be able to circulate more or less freely as a member of the resistance movement. Here is a wide-open field for the activities of the counterfeit section.

Congregations of more than ten persons will be prohibited. Clubs and associations will be prohibited. Court-martials and quick trials will be initiated. It will be announced publically that anyone apprehended with a weapon will be shot on the spot.

All house owners and janitors are responsible that house doors, cellar and attic doors are closed at all times. Strangers may only enter after a check. The house owner or janitor will be jointly responsible for any hostile acts committed by these strangers against the occupation forces from their house (basic rule: each is to watch and shadow the other out of fear and self-preservation).

All shutters and blinds facing the street must be open. However, all windows must be closed. Patrols will fire into open windows without any warning.

c. Proclamation of siege:

A state of siege will be advertised by posters, loudspeakers, trucks, radios and leaflets dropped from planes.

Reconnaissance prior to the attack

The occupation forces will conduct a reconnaissance prior to cleaning up an area of unrest or putting down an uprising. This reconnaissance will not only concern the military sector but the political as well.

You must fight this enemy reconnaissance. However, your mission will be made more difficult by the fact that enemy reconnaissance elements will work primarily in civilian clothes. They will be composed of members of the political police (State Security Service), officers of the occupation army, followers and collaborators.

The enemy will, of course, not work in patrols but will work for the most part alone.

The reconnaissance is to clear the following points:

a. Political situation:

What sympathies, what support and what practical cooperation do the active insurgents have among the masses of the population?

What is the attitude of their own civilian government, i.e., puppet administration, composed of former members of the Fifth Column? Is it still "firm" or has it reached the opinion that the "moment" has come "to change sides"?

b. Military situation:

Evaluate the number of weapons and amount of ammunition available to the insurgents. Determine if they have heavy infantry weapons such as machine guns and mortars, and anti-tank weapons such as mines, rocket launchers, and AT rifles.

Do they make a good and cohesive impression or is their organization loose and improvised? Are they cleverly led according to military principles which would indicate that they have former officers and NCO's leading them or do they act like amateurs?

Do they build obstacles? Do they occupy positions? Are there good roads of access for entering the town? What is a rough estimate (border lines) of area of unrest?

At least find out roughly in what part of the city the headquarters of the uprising is located.

You will see at once from the above that the reconnaissance of the political situation almost takes precedence over the military sector; at least it ranks equally important. Consequently, the enemy reconnaissance elements should be able to judge human beings and present matter-of-fact opinions in their delicate missions. Since they are party fanatics, however, they will see everything in a different light. The ability to make critical judgments is mostly lacking in them since they were educated according to a strict doctrine. As a result, reconnaissance results will at least lack something in the political sector which is of advantage to you, i.e., poor estimate of situation by enemy leaders.

Along with the reconnaissance the enemy will attempt to secure plans or maps of the city. These will render the enemy good services during city fights due to his lack of knowledge of the area and he will attempt to procure these in quantities. You must remove them. A systematic collection of these plans is one of the first missions of a careful preparation for an uprising. By means of specially designated sections you will have these plans removed from the following places: city planning office (surface and subsurface constructions), book stores, stationery stores, and official map sales stores.

The securing of plans on the sewage system also is part of this operation. (See also booklet entitled "Fighting Techniques," Vol. II, page 32-35, with illustrations and directives on the fight in the sewage system, published by the Central Secretariat of the Swiss NCO Association, Biel).

Based upon the results of the reconnaissance, the occupation forces will establish a plan (operations plan). It basically has two possibilities:

Planned, rather demonstrative entry.	Surprise, raid-like attack.
This is to serve to cause people to come to their senses. Mostly used during rather advanced unrests. Will give you time for counter-measures.	Will leave you no time for counter-measures. Mostly used during weak uprisings. Occupation forces must improvise and risk the danger of repercussions.

The enemy will commit as large a troop contingent as possible so as not to suffer any defeat for such an event would greatly enhance the insurgent movement and drive many undecided and careful persons into the arms of the active fighters.

Sealing off an area of unrest by the occupation forces

a. General

Armored and mechanized troops encircle the city by closing off the main arterial roads, in order to prevent an escape of the insurgents, and to prevent help and supplies from reaching the insurgents from the outside.

Individual armored raiding groups will attack along main routes in the direction of the center of the city in order to occupy individual, important points and split up the insurgents into several, separate fighting groups.

Most of the enemy infantry will comb the various city sections, blocks and buildings slowly and systematically.

A motorized main reserve will be kept ready outside the town in order to counter attempts to break out, relieve tired units, replace

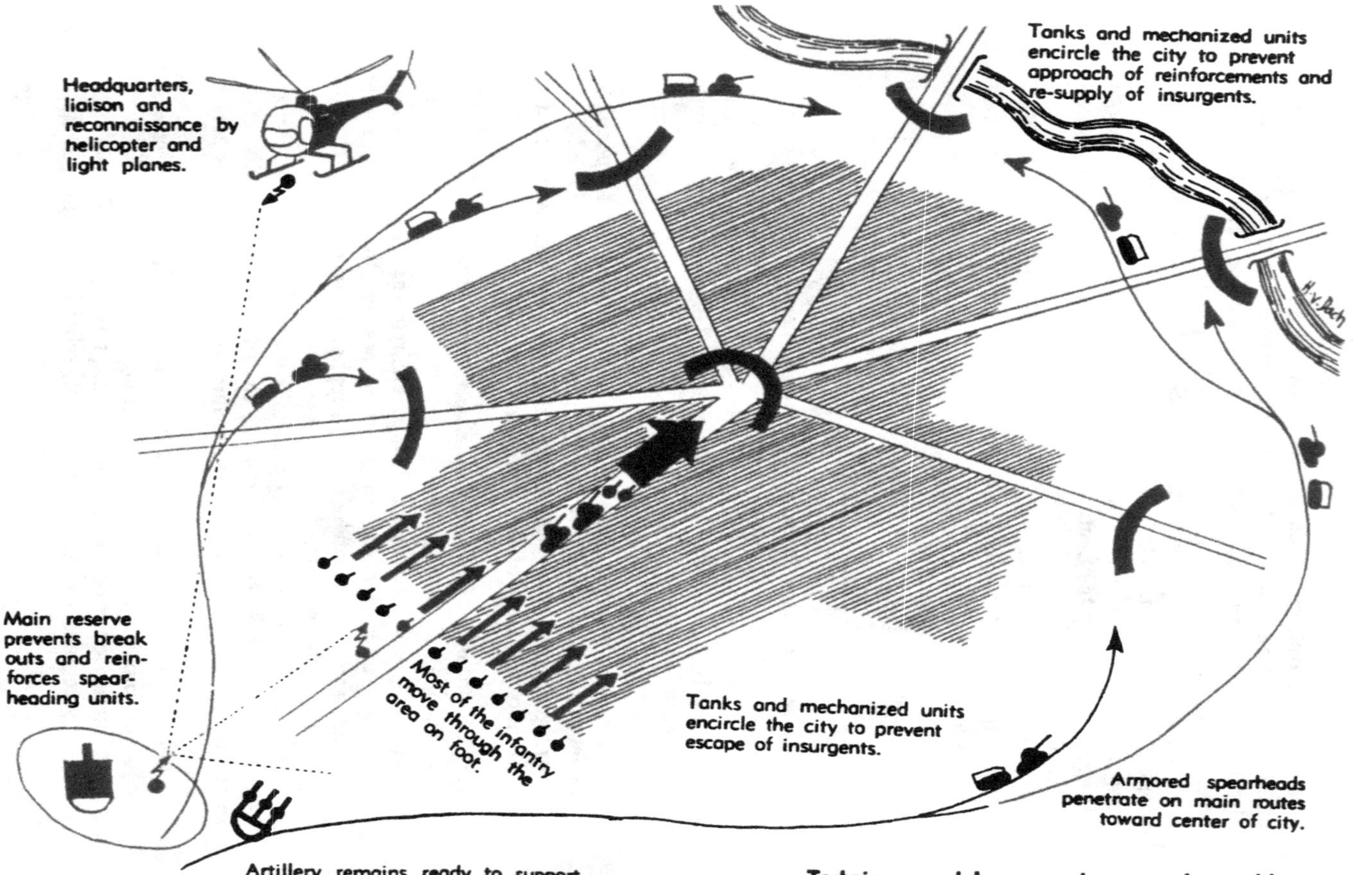

Techniques used by enemy in suppressing uprisings.

losses, reinforce, if necessary, the spearhead units, and to eliminate later especially tenaciously defended pockets of resistance. Coordination and direction of the operation will be facilitated by radio, helicopter and light planes.

b. Detailed organization

The occupation powers will organize basically their units as follows: "forces to seal off"; outer perimeter; inner perimeter; and "mopping-up forces."

All forces (military, party militia, regular police forces, State Security Service) are placed under one command.

Chief of entire operation. High military commander, perhaps police general of State Security Service, NKVD.	If the commanding officer is from the military, then he will be a party "follower" who is absolutely true to the party line.
Chief of perimeter organization Military Party militia Police	Chief of mopping-up operation. Military State Security Service

"Outer Perimeter force": Will prevent unauthorized traffic in the area of the uprising (rerouting traffic). Will protect mopping-up forces against operations from the outside, i.e., attacks from guerrilla units supporting the insurgents. Main element of the outer sealing-off force is the party militia supported by individual policemen who regulate traffic and "screen" persons and vehicles passing through. Individual tanks and infantry elements of the occupation power serve as a battle-ready back-up force. The "outer seal-off force" only blocks main routes of access at the periphery of the area of uprising. This is a tight little net which can be easily bypassed by using secondary roads.

"Inner Perimeter force": Will prevent escape of insurgents. Thus is as tight and close as possible. Main tactical element is the infantry. Areas with wide field of fire (parks, canals, large streets, open squares) are selected to save on personnel for the sealing-off operation since combing the area thoroughly requires many personnel.

"Mopping-up forces": Raiding elements—infantry and individual armored personnel carriers—will knock out pockets of resistance. Fire support elements will assist the advance of the raiding elements, i.e., self-propelled guns, tanks, mortars, machine guns. Search detachments will consist of infantry, as well as specialists of the State Security Service. Reserves will support the attack as well as guard and transport prisoners.

The enemy assembly area

The enemy likes to use open, easily controllable areas (RR marshalling yards, larger inconnecting parks, etc.) as assembly areas. He will be able to do this since you do not possess any heavy weapons (artillery, planes, mortars) to smash known assembly areas and troop concentrations. Assembly in open and easily controlled area will make it easier for the enemy to assemble and organize his units, brief subordinate unit commanders on the terrain and position heavy

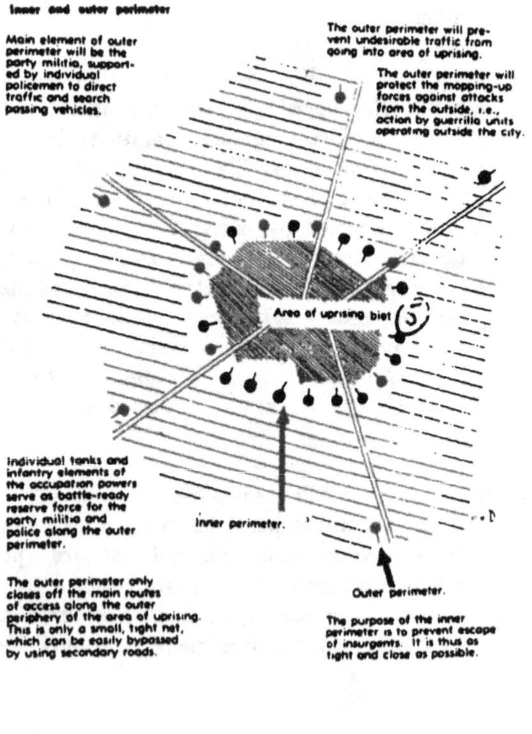

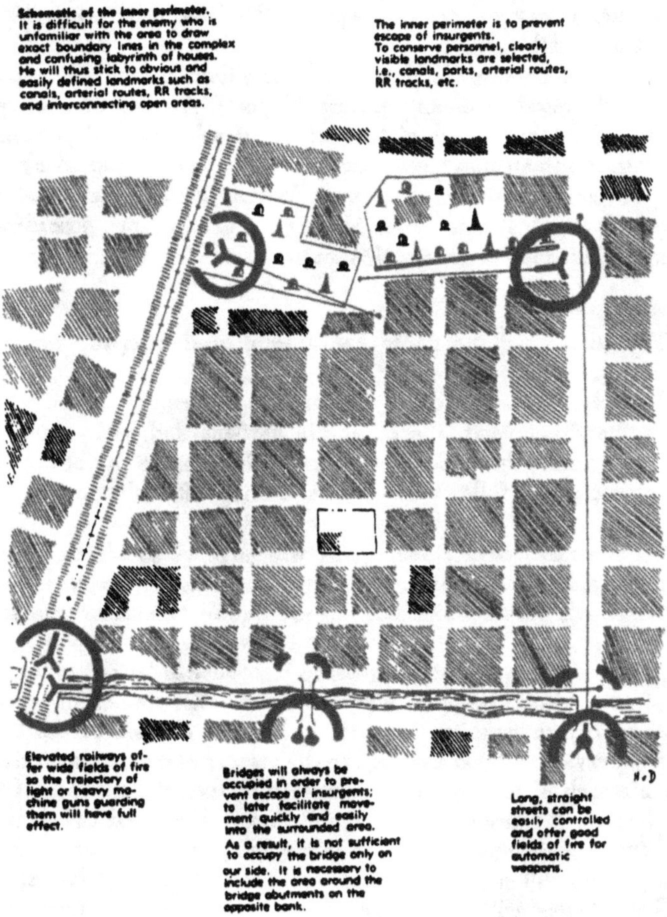

support weapons (guns, mortars) which in spite of "high-angle fire" will not be able to be effective from narrow streets.

Thus remember: Large open areas near your defensive front are dangerous. As long as you still have freedom of movement you must position yourself in such a manner that such areas (parks, open spaces, railroad tracks) are to your rear. Where you have been unable to do this your few mortars must be able to concentrate on these points.

Point of penetration on enemy

The tactical rule in city fighting is to select the point of penetration in such a way so that the depth of the area to be penetrated is as short as possible.

You must continually enter on your situation map any reports about newly installed enemy sealing-off posts. As time goes on you will obtain a pretty good picture of the development of the inner perimeter. You can now easily see where the area occupied by you shows the smallest depth. You must assume rather safely that the enemy will attack at this point. Make your preparations accordingly by increasing observation at this point, relocating reserves, etc.

Advance in streets

The enemy will normally use a reinforced company for each main street.

Two platoons will probably advance together next to each other; one on the street itself, the other via gardens and backyards. The enemy will select that side of the street which offers the best cover. The third platoon follows as reserve, sealing off and searching the area.

On the main street, one squad will advance in file to the left and right along the houses. One squad will follow as reserve on the side which provides the most cover. One or two tanks or assault guns will advance with the infantry to provide fire support.

At least one squad of the reserve platoon will be committed on both sides to search the houses passed by the lead platoon to prevent a flare-up of the fight in the rear. Individual officials of the State Security Service are also assigned to the reserve platoon as specialists. Since a search of houses requires more time than the advance of the lead element, the reserve platoon will dictate the speed of advance. When the lead element engages in a fire fight, personnel further back in the column will step behind and into houses to prevent losses.

The advance will halt at each street intersecting the direction of advance and the unit will regroup. You can see by the above that the advance of the enemy will be very difficult and, above all, time-consuming.

Eliminating barricades

The enemy will attempt to destroy barricades from a great distance by using his superior heavy weapons, i.e., tanks, assault guns, direct artillery fire.

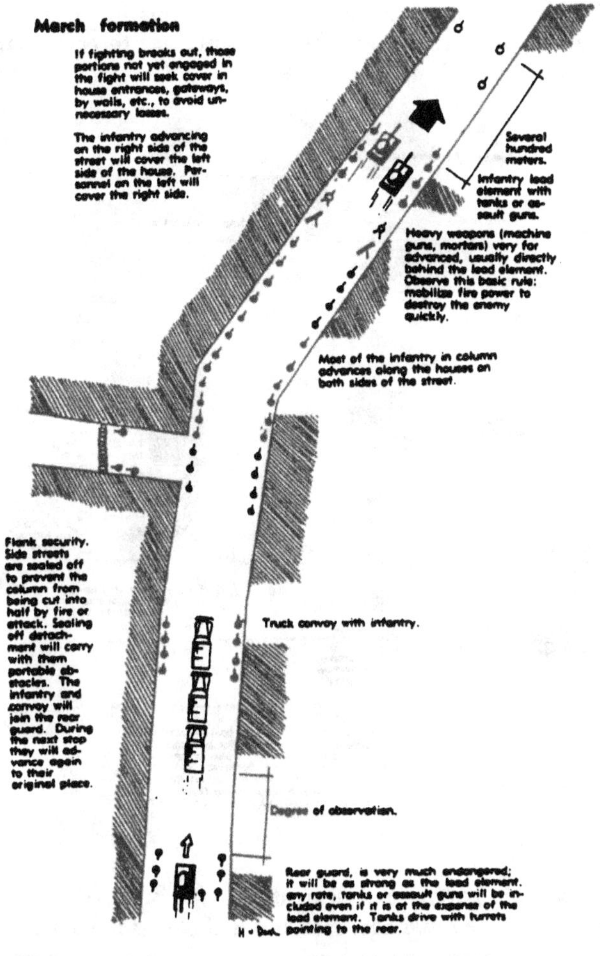

Where you have so installed your barricades in such a manner to prevent this, the enemy will never attack the barricade frontally but advance to the left and right through the houses with infantry (raiding parties). The barricade will then fall almost by itself.

Clearing large buildings by the occupation forces

The entire area concerned will be surrounded. Routes of access will be closed off by barbed wire (concertina wire) and soldiers with submachine guns. Tanks will drive up and guard the buildings concerned with machine gun and canon. Automatic weapons will be positioned in and on the neighboring buildings to control the roofs of the target area.

Elimination of barricades and road blocks

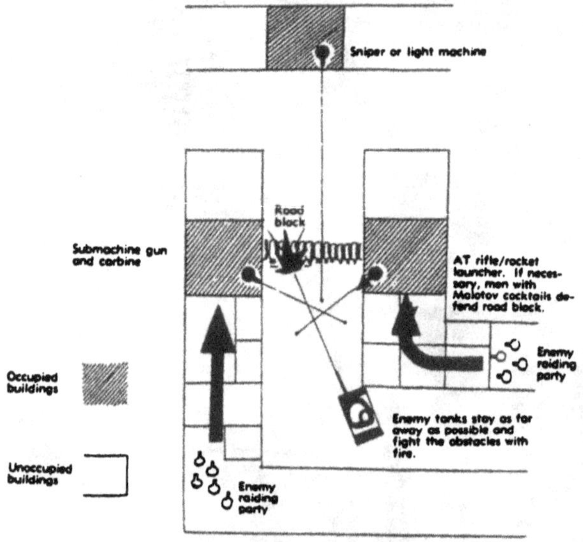

The enemy infantry assault parties advance from house to house toward the barricade by means of breaking through walls, always advancing through rooms farthest from the streets. They thus cannot be fired on through windows by snipers in neighboring houses. The advance will take considerably time but the enemy will avoid losses.

An assault party, i.e., elements of the State Security Service, penetrates into the buildings, searches and cleans them out systematically. Suspicious persons and prisoners will be taken away immediately. Trucks and officials of the State Security Service will be kept ready for the transportation of prisoners. A reserve element will wait under cover in order to handle arrested persons or reinforce the assault element. Loudspeakers will broadcast announcements and appeals to the "enemy." Searchlights will be positiioned to assist the operation at night, if necessary.

Operations of superior enemy in quelling an uprising.

Tanks drive up and watch the building in question.

Routes of access will be closed off by barbed wire and posts.

Assault elements penetrate and den mop-up buildings.

Reserves are kept ready.

Loudspeakers and searchlights are put in position.

Elements of the State Security Service in civilian clothes and detachments of occupation troops work together.

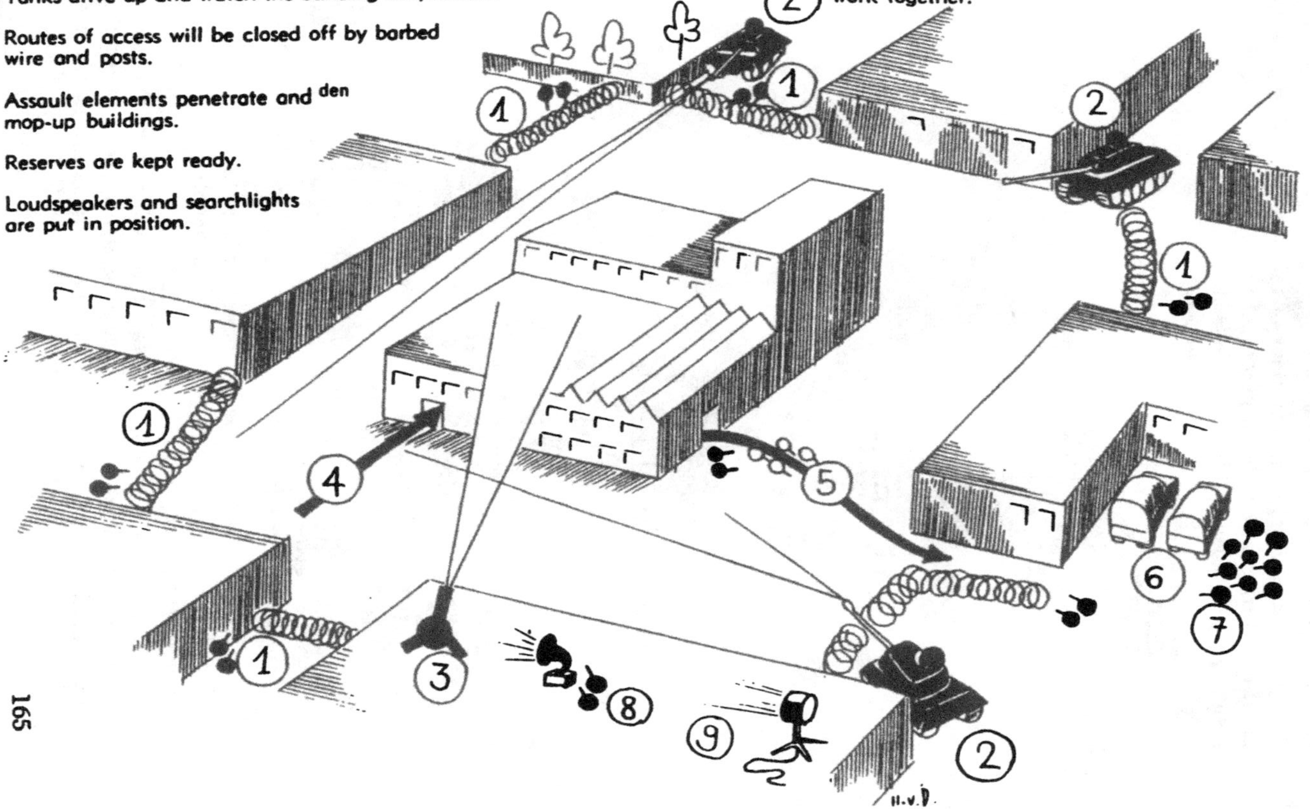

Clearing an open area by the enemy

To disperse mass demonstrations of the desperate population in front of government buildings, party and administration seats, monuments, etc., the enemy will do the following:

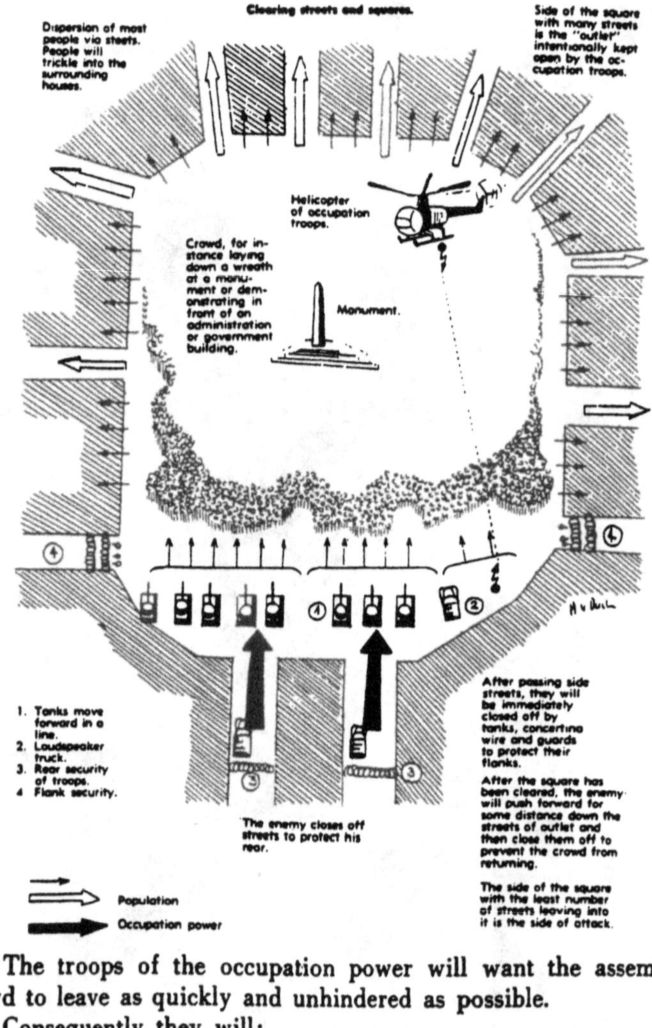

The troops of the occupation power will want the assembled crowd to leave as quickly and unhindered as possible.

Consequently they will:

a. Give orders through loudspeaker trucks to have the doors of the surrounding houses open, but to close the windows facing the square, thus allowing a considerable portion of the crowd to disperse into the houses but at the same time make it difficult for the escapees to fire from closed windows upon troops and police.

b. Keep many streets open on purpose to provide the crowds with avenues of escape.

c. Clear the square from only one side, selecting that side from which the least streets lead into the square.

In order to clear the square, the enemy will use primarily tanks, armored personnel carriers or at least trucks. They will advance slowly in one line at consistent pace—often with one flank slightly ahead which facilitates observation—and thus push back the crowd.

Infantry will be mounted on the vehicles to prevent the crowd from tearing down antennas, tools, flags, etc., from the vehicles or throw Molotov cocktails at them.

Behind the tanks follow reserve elements at some distance with trucks. They have the mission:

To close off immediately side streets passed by the tanks with movable wire obstacles and guards to prevent portions of the crowd from returning and attacking the rear of the clearing elements.

To take charge of persons arrested and transport them to the rear in trucks.

Occupation of a city after uprisings are suppressed

After entry and clearing operations are completed, "restricted areas" will be established which will support the occupation troops. In these areas the occupation troops will be strictly separated from the population. This way the troops can be protected and removed from the political influence of the population.

Areas adjacent to "restricted areas" will be patrolled by infantry and tanks. Infantry patrols will hide in armored personnel carriers, if possible, or at least on trucks carrying machine guns.

Strong points will be established in the adjacent areas to support the patrols. They will be few in number so as not to disperse forces, but will be able to withstand attack.

They are always installed in solid buildings which can be easily defended. Often they will be situated in places which have to be guarded anyhow, i.e., power companies, arsenals, bridges, etc.

Patrols will be led by officers. Only within the immediate vicinity of the restricted area (several hundred meters) are these patrols of squad strength. Otherwise, they will consist at least of one platoon with machine gun mounted on a truck.

Officers leading the patrols are usually the best the enemy has to offer (read: "the most ruthless" and "trigger happy").

Officers are above all to prevent any contact between the population and the soldiers and to make sure that the latter are not disarmed by the population. They will not refrain from firing even in the presence of women and children.

Patrols are especially dangerous since they will open fire quickly out of fear; at any rate, sooner than a large closed unit. The smaller a patrol and the farther away from the restricted area, the sooner it will make use of its weapons.

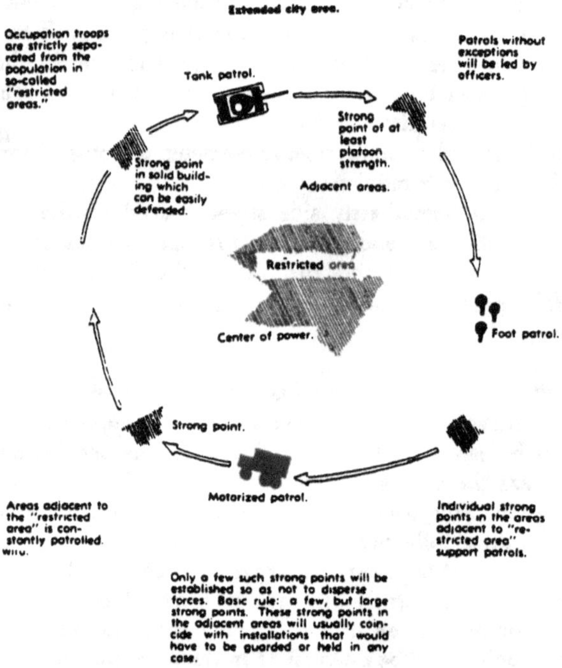

Individual guards along the periphery of the "restricted area" will be replaced as soon as possible by barbed wire entanglements. This will conserve personnel and will be even more effective.

Individual guards are always positioned at least 30 meters behind the barbed wire entanglement to prevent them from talking to the population. If they have to yell to speak with the people they will soon stop. Even more so since comrades and superiors may be able to listen to what is being said. As a result guards are automatically removed from the political influence and distraction of the population. Thus the ideological gap is once more guaranteed.

Normally a sign will warn against trespassing beyond the barbed wire entanglement. Anyone attempting to cross the line will be fired upon ruthlessly and without warning.

Disarmament

A certain cut-off date will be set for turning over weapons, ammunition, explosives, and hand grenades; until then people are assured of not being punished if they turn over these weapons. This guarantee will be adhered to at least in the beginning so as not to frighten anyone away.

Patrol

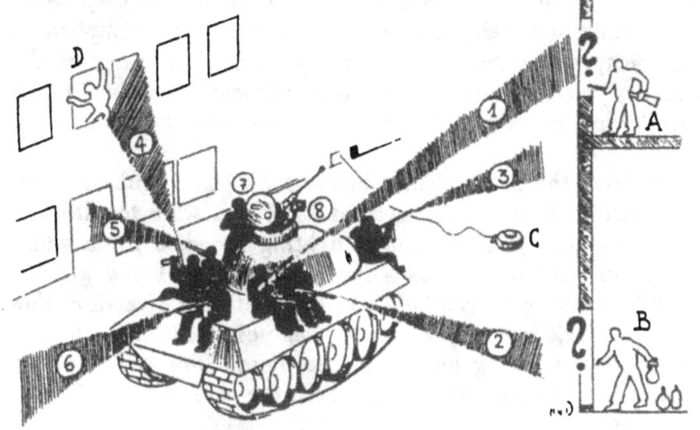

1. Observes to the right and up for roof and window snipers.
2. Observes down and right for individuals with Molotov cocktails.
3. Observes to the front and down for mines.
4. Observes to the left and up.
5. Observes down and left.
6. Observes to the rear.
7. Patrol leader, usually an officer, works together with the tank commander in the turret.
8. Tank commander mans the AA gun and observes to the front and up.

A. Roof or window sniper.
B. Man with Molotov cocktails.
C. Mines.
D. Curious individuals.

Any open window or open door will be fired upon without any warning.
The farther patrols are from their strong points and the weaker they are the more dangerous they are since they will fire quickly out of fear and nervousness.

Should you be so trusting and turn over your weapons you will be put on a "black list" in spite of everything. The enemy will always need hostages or forced laborers later on (read: "work slaves") and will gladly make use of the "black lists." You see once again that you cannot escape his net and had better die fighting.

After the deadline, raids coupled with house searches and street checks will be conducted.

During a street check, certain streets are closed off all of a sudden and pedestrians are searched for weapons. Vehicles and contents are searched.

There are many ways to dispose of incriminating material when caught in a street check. If you carry a pistol, explosives, hand grenade, underground newspaper, or leaflets on your person, you must act quickly. During the first few minutes after the street has been blocked off, general confusion will reign; you must take advantage of this. About ten minutes later, the enemy will begin to collect all pedestrians "caught in the net" and line them up in a formation (rows, columns of two) to be able to guard them better. Once part of the formation, you will hardly be able to dispose of the incriminating material. Your task will be even more complicated since the enemy has previously sent in agents and informers of the State Security Service into the area who allowed themselves to be caught as "harmless pedestrians" and who now discreetly watch the crowd.

If you carry the material in a briefcase, a small suitcase or in a tool box put it down on the ground as if you were too lazy to carry it any longer. Stand next to it fighting boredom for a while and then attempt to walk away as if you forgot it. If you are accompanied by a friend he can help you by creating a diversion. For instance he can look excitedly at a roof, then point at it and call out: "There! Someone is doing gymnastics up there! Now he is gone!" In the confusion you will move away from the case in order "to be able to see better."

Smaller objects such as pistols, hand grenades, bundles of leaflets, single newspapers, can be disposed of in the following manner. Sit down on the curb near the hole. Several friends may be able to stand around you to give you cover and attempt to direct the attention of others elsewhere. Slide the incriminating object into the sewer.

A garden fence is also very good. Lean against it as if bored. Pull out a package of cigarettes and light one. Put the lighter into the bag in which you have the material. When you remove your hand withdraw the object at the same time, hold your hands behind your back and let it slide into the garden through the fence. Even here friends may be able to help you by providing cover.

Attempt later on to recover the object thrown away—especially in the case of weapons. Let at least three days go by. The enemy may have rigged a trap.

If you are an innocent bystander and notice that people are

trying to hide objects, it is your duty to help them as much as you can by ignoring their actions, or by contributing in attempts to distract attention from them.

Search of a block of houses

On the evening before or during the night, a scout in civilian clothes (official of the State Security Service, military, etc.) will conduct a reconnaissance to determine good routes of approach, roadblocks needed, number of personnel required.

Approach, encirclement and blocking off the area will be done at dawn. The enemy will conduct this operation as quickly as possible to prevent you from taking counter measures such as organizing resistance, hiding out, escaping, etc.

House-to-house search

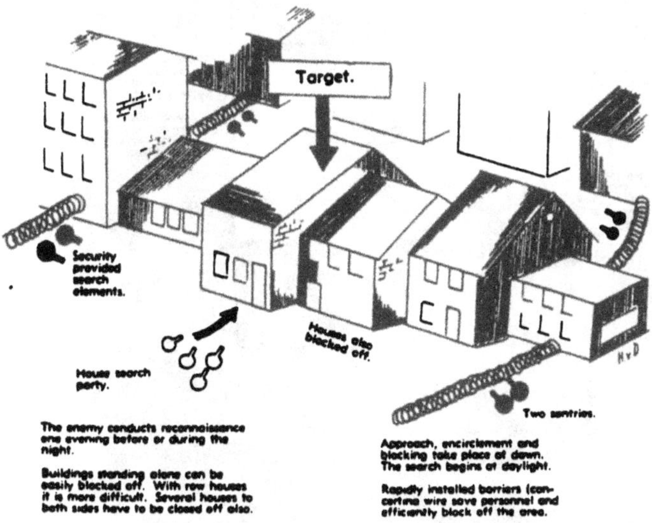

The house search begins at daylight before people go to work (early shift).

Whenever possible, movable barriers (concertina wire) will be used to conserve personnel. The barrier is to prevent a coming and going of persons from one side to the other. At the same time the enemy provides security for his search elements by using barriers.

Buildings standing alone (villas, etc.) do not offer any particular difficulties. Row houses, however, are more complicated. Here he has at the same time to close off several buildings on both sides of the "target."

Normally, an infantry squad of ten to twelve men will be accompanied by one or two members of the State Security Service. Two sentries will be stationed immediately in the attic to prevent escapes via roofs. One guard will be posted in the stairwell on each floor; he will watch the doors. Three men will be on the bottom floor. One each will guard the front and rear house entrance, while the third man will guard the entrance to the basement.

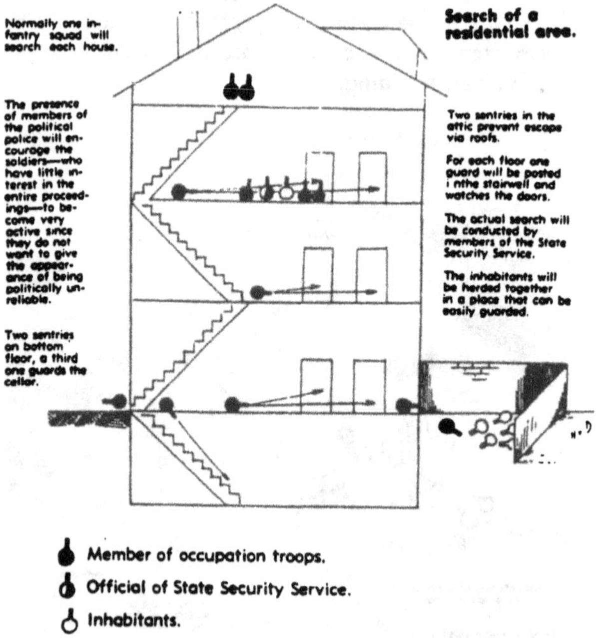

Search of a residential area.

As a rule, all inhabitants will be herded together in a place which can be easily guarded (yard, corner of wall). The owner or janitor must indicate if all are present, who is missing and who does not belong among the inhabitants.

Then the inhabitants are called up individually when it is their turn to have their apartments searched. Doors which cannot be opened will be broken open. The systematic search requires a lot of time. In this case the specialists of the State Security Service will render good services in various respects.

The presence alone of the hated and feared organ of the political police will have a paralyzing and intimidating effect upon the inhabitants.

The individual soldier, on the inside entirely disinterested in the whole operation, is forced to greatest activity and harshness by the presence of the representatives of the regime if he does not want to run the risk of being considered politically unreliable.

The following will be searched carefully: small water tanks of the various types of toilets, closets, suitcases, boxes, stoves, stove pipes (suitable weapons cache), chimneys (hiding places for persons), beds, etc. In addition, they will check the floors to see if they have been tampered with.

Heaps of rubble, waste, wood or coal piles in basements and yards will be probed.

Closing Remarks

If two enemies fight each other to the last—and this is always the case when an ideology is involved (religion is part of it)—guerrilla warfare and civilian resistance will inevitably break out in the final phase.

The military expert who undervalues or even disregards guerrilla warfare makes a mistake since he does not take into consideration the strength of the heart.

The last, and admittedly, most cruel battle will be fought by civilians. It will be conducted under the fear of deportation, of execution, and concentration camps.

We must and will win this battle since each Swiss male and female in particular believe in the innermost part of their hearts—even if they are too shy and sober in everyday life to admit or even to speak about it—in the old and yet very up-to-date saying:

"Death rather than slavery!"

Bern, March 17, 1958 The Author

CPSIA information can be obtained
at www.ICGtesting.com
Printed in the USA
FSHW012115180221